George MacDonald

The Disciple

And Other Poems

George MacDonald

The Disciple
And Other Poems

ISBN/EAN: 9783744712125

Printed in Europe, USA, Canada, Australia, Japan

Cover: Foto ©Thomas Meinert / pixelio.de

More available books at **www.hansebooks.com**

THE DISCIPLE
AND OTHER POEMS

THE DISCIPLE

AND OTHER POEMS

By GEORGE MACDONALD, LL.D.

A NEW EDITION

LONDON
CHATTO & WINDUS
1897

CONTENTS.

POEMS:—

	Page
A Story of the Sea-Shore	3
To Lady Noel Byron	33
To the Same	34
To Aurelio Saffi	35
The Disciple	39

THE GOSPEL WOMEN:—

I.—The Mother Mary	103
II.—The Woman that lifted up her Voice	118
III.—The Mother of Zebedee's Children	120
IV.—The Syrophenician Woman	123
V.—The Widow of Nain	126
VI.—The Woman whom Satan had Bound	130
VII.—The Woman who came behind Him in the Crowd	133
VIII.—The Widow with the Two Mites	135

CONTENTS.

THE GOSPEL WOMEN :—*continued.*

		Page
IX.—The Women who ministered unto Him.		137
X.—Pilate's Wife		138
XI.—The Woman of Samaria		140
XII.—Mary Magdalene		142
XIII.—The Woman in the Temple		145
XIV.—Martha		150
XV.—Mary		153
XVI.—The Woman that was a Sinner		158

A BOOK OF SONNETS :—

The Burnt Offering.	165
The Unseen Face.	167
Concerning Jesus	168
A Memorial of Africa	186
A. M. D.	188
To Garibaldi	189
To S. F. S.	190

ORGAN SONGS :—

| To A. J. Scott | 193 |
| Light | 196 |

CONTENTS.

ORGAN SONGS:—*continued.*

	Page
To A. J. Scott	213
I would I were a Child	215
A Prayer for the Past	219
Longing	229
I know what Beauty is	232
Sympathy	235
The Thank-Offering	238
Prayer	240
Rest	241
O do not leave Me	246
Blessed are the Meek, for they shall inherit the Earth	247
Hymn for a Sick Girl	250
A Christmas Carol for 1862	252
A Christmas Carol	256
The Sleepless Jesus	258
The Children's Heaven	261
Rejoice	265
The Grace of Grace	267
Antiphony	269
Dorcas	273

ORGAN SONGS:—*continued.*

    MARRIAGE SONG

    BLIND BARTIMEUS

    COME UNTO ME

    MORNING HYMN

    NOONTIDE

    EVENING HYMN

    THE HOLY MIDNIGHT

POEMS.

A STORY OF THE SEA-SHORE.

INTRODUCTION.

I SOUGHT the long clear twilights of my home,
Far in the pale-blue skies and slaty seas,
What time the sunset dies not utterly,
But withered to a ghost-like stealthy gleam,
Round the horizon creeps the short-lived night,
And changes into sunrise in a swoon.
I found my home in homeliness unchanged:
The love that made it home, unchangeable,
Received me as a child, and all was well.

My ancient summer-heaven, borne on the hills,
Once more embraced me; and once more the vale,
So often sighed for in the far-off nights,
Rose on my bodily vision, and, behold!
In nothing had the fancy mocked the fact:
The hasting streams went garrulous as of old;
The resting flowers in silence uttered more;
The blue hills rose and dwelt alone in heaven;
Householding Nature from her treasures brought
Things old and new, the same yet not the same,
For all was holier, lovelier than before.
And best of all, once more I paced the fields
With him whose love had made me long for God—
So good a father that needs-must I sought
A better still, Father of him and me.

Once on a day, my cousin Frank and I
Sat swiftly borne behind the dear white mare

Which oft had carried me in by-gone days
Along the lonely paths of moorland hills;
But now we sought the coast, where deep waves foam
Gainst rocks that lift their dark fronts to the north.
Beside me sat a girl, on whose kind face
I had not looked for many a changeful year,
But the old friendship straightway blossomed new.
The heavens were sunny, and the earth was green
The harebells large, in gathered groups along
The grassy borders, of a tender blue
Transparent as the sky, haunted with wings
Of many butterflies, as blue as they;
And as we talked and talked without restraint,
Brought near by memories of days that were
And therefore are for ever, by the joy
Of motion through a warm and shining air,
By the glad sense of freedom and like thoughts

And by the bond of friendship with the dead,
She told the tale which here I tell again.

I had returned to childish memories,
Asking her if she knew a castle old,
Whose masonry, all worn away above,
Yet faced the sea-cliff up, and met the waves:
'Twas one of my child-marvels; for, each year,
We turned our backs upon the ripening corn,
And sought some village on the desert shore;
And nigh this ruin, was that I loved the best.

For oh, the riches of that little port!—
Down almost to the beach, where a high wall
Inclosed them, came the gardens of a lord,
Free to the visitor with foot restrained—
His shady walks, his ancient trees of state;
His river, which, outside the wall, with cour--
Indefinite, went dreaming o'er the sands,

And lost itself in finding out the sea,
But inside, bore grave swans, white splendours—
    crept
Under the fairy leap of a wire bridge,
Vanished in leaves, and came again where lawns
Lay verdurous, and the peacock's plumy heaven
Bore azure suns with green and golden rays.
It was my childish Eden ; for the skies
Were loftier in that garden, and the clouds
More summer-gracious, edged with broader white ;
And when they rained, it was a golden rain
That sparkled as it fell—an odorous rain.
And then its wonder-heart !—a little room,
Half-hollowed in the side of a steep hill :
The hill was with a circular temple crowned,
A landmark to far seas ; the room below
Was clouded ever in the gentle night
Of a luxuriant ivy, and its door,
Half-filled with rainbow hues of colcured glass,

Opened into the bosom of the hill.
Never to sesame of mine that door
Gave up its sanctuary; but through the glass
Gazing with reverent curiosity,
I saw a little chamber, round and high,
Which to behold was to escape the heat,
And bathe in coolness of the eye and brain.
All was a dusky green; for on one side,
A window, half-blind with ivy manifold,
Whose leaves, like heads of gazers, climbed to the
    top,
Gave all the light, and all the light that came
Through the thick veil, was green, oh, kindest hue!
But the heart has a heart, and here was one;
For in the midst, the ever more of all,
On a low column stood, white, cold, and clear,
A marble woman. Who she was I know not—
A Psyche, or a Silence, or an Echo.
Pale, undefined, a silvery shadow, still,

In one lone chamber of my memory,
She is a power upon me, as of old.

  But ah! to dream there through hot summer days,
In coolness shrouded and sea-murmurings,
Forgot by all till twilight shades grew dark!
To find half-hidden in the hollowed wall,
A nest of tales, quaint volumes such as dreams
Hoard up in bookshops dim in tortuous streets!
That wondrous marble woman evermore
Filling the gloom with calm delirium
Of radiated whiteness, as I read!—
The fancied joy, too plenteous for its cup,
O'erflowed, and turned to sadness as it fell.

  But the gray ruin on the shattered shore,
Not the green refuge in the bowering hill,
Drew forth our talk that day. For, as I said,

I asked her if she knew it. She replied,
" I know it well. A woman used to live
In one of its low vaults, my mother says."
" I came once on a turret stair," I said,
" Leading from level of the ground above
To a low-vaulted room within the rock,
Whence through a small square opening you look
    forth
Wide o'er the sea ; but the dim-sounding waves
Are many feet below, and shrunk in size
To a great ripple." "'Twas not there," she
    said—
" Not in that room half up the cliff, but one
Below, within the margin of spring tides ;
So that when tides and northern winds are high,
'Tis more an ocean-cave than castle-vault."
And then she told me all she knew of her.

It was a simple tale, with facts but few :

She clomb one sunny hill, gazed once abroad,
Then slowly sank to pace a dreary plain.
Alas! how many such are told by night,
In fisher-cottages along the shore!

Farewell, old summer-day! I turn aside
To tell my story, interwoven with thoughts
Born of its sorrow; for I dare not think
A woman at the mercy of a sea.

THE STORY.

Aye as it listeth blows the listless wind,
Swelling great sails, and bending lordly masts,
Or scaring shadow-waves o'er fields of corn,
And hunting lazy clouds across the sky:
Now, like a white cloud o'er another sky,
It blows a tall brig from the harbour's mouth,
Out 'mid the high-tossed heads of broken waves,
And hoverings of long-pinioned arrowy birds.

With clouds and birds and sails and broken crests,
All space is full of spots of fluttering white,
And yet one sailor knows that handkerchief
Waved wet with tears, and heavy in the wind.
Blow, wind! draw out the cord that binds the twain;
Draw, for thou canst not break the lengthening cord.
Blow, wind! yet gently; gently blow, fair wind!
And let love's vision slowly, gently die;
Let the bright sails all solemn-slowly pass,
And linger ghost-like o'er the vanished hull,
With a white farewell to her straining eyes;
For never more in morning's level beams,
Will those sea-shadowing sails, storm-stained and worn,
From the gray-billowed north come dancing in;
And never, gliding home 'neath starry skies,
Over the dark of the dim-glancing sea,

Will the great ship send forth a herald cry
Of home-come sailors, into sleeping streets.
Blow gently, wind! blow slowly, gentle wind!
    Weep not yet, maiden; 'tis not yet thy hour.
Why shouldst thou weep before thy time is come?
Go to thy work; break into song sometimes,
Song dying slow-forgotten, in the lapse
Of dreamy thought, ere natural pause ensue;
Or broken sudden when the eager heart
Hurries the ready eye to north and east.
Sing, maiden, while thou canst, ere yet the truth,
Slow darkening on thee, choke the founts of song.

    The weeks went by. Oft leaving household work,
With bare arms and uncovered head she clomb
The landward slope of the prophetic hill;
From whose green head, as from the verge of time,
Far out on the eternity of waves,
Shading her hope-rapt eyes, seer-like she gazed,

If from the Hades of the nether world,
Slow climbing up the round side of the earth,
Haply her prayers were drawing his tardy sails
Over the threshold of the far horizon;—
Drawing her sailor home, to celebrate
With holy rites of family and church
The apotheosis of maidenhood.
   Months passed; he came not; and a shadowy fear,
Long haunting the horizon of her soul,
In deeper gloom and sharper form drew nigh;
And growing in bulk, possessed her atmosphere,
And lost all shape, because it filled all space,
And reached beyond the bounds of consciousness;
But in sudden incarnations darting swift
From out its infinite a gulfy stare
Of terror blank, and hideous emptiness,
And widowhood or ever wedding-day.

On granite ridge, and chalky cliff, and pier,
Far built into the waves along our shores,
Maidens have stood since ever ships went forth;
The same pain at the heart; the same slow mist
Clouding the eye; the same fixed longing look,
As if the soul had gone out and left the door
Wide open—gone to lean and peep and peer
Over the awful edge, where voidness sinks
Sheer to oblivion—that horizon-line
Over whose edge he vanished—came no more.
O God, why are our souls, lone helpless seas,
Tortured with such immitigable storm?
What is this love, that now on angel wing
Sweeps us amid the stars in passionate calm;
And now with demon arms fast cincturing,
Drops us, through all gyrations of keen pain,
Down the black vortex, till the giddy whirl
Gives fainting respite to the ghastly brain?
O happy they for whom the Possible

Opens its gates of madness, and becomes
The Real around them! those to whom henceforth
There is but one to-morrow, the next morn,
Their wedding day, ever one step removed;
The husband's foot ever upon the verge
Of the day's threshold, in a lasting dream!
Such madness may be but a formless faith—
A chaos which the breath of God will blow
Into an ordered world of seed and fruit?
Shall not the Possible become the Real?
God sleeps not when he makes his daughters dream.
Shall not the morrow dawn which leads at last
The maiden-ghost, confused and half awake
Into the land whose shadows are our dreams
Thus questioning we stand upon the shore,
And gaze across into the Unrevealed.

   Upon its visible symbol gazed the girl,

Till earth behind her ceased, and sea was all,
Possessing eyes and brain and shrinking soul;
So smooth, because all mouth to swallow up,
And cover the invisible with blue smile;
A still monotony of greed and loss,
Its only voice an endless, dreary song
Of wailing, and of craving from the shore;
A low dull dirge that ever rose and died,
Recurring without pause or change or close
Like one verse chaunted ever in sleepless brain.
Down to the shore it drew her, drew her down,
Like witch's spell, that fearful endless moan;
For somewhere in the green abyss below,
His body, in the centre of the moan,
Obeyed the motions whence the moaning grew;
Now in a circle slow revolved, and now
Swaying like wind-swung bell, or swept along
Hither and thither, idly to and fro,
In heedless wandering through the heedless sea.

The fascination drew her onward still;
On to the ridgy rocks that seaward ran,
And out along their furrows and jagged backs,
To the last lonely point where the green mass
Arose and sank, heaved slow and forceful. There
She shuddered and recoiled. Then, for a time
From that hour, to and fro between she went,
'Twixt shore and ocean alternating—ever
Drawn to the greedy lapping lip, and ever
Once more repelled, with terror sudden stung;
For there the heartless, miserable depth
Lay in close wait, with horror's glittering eye
Enticing her to its green gulfing maw.

   At length a faint hope grew, that, once the prey
Of the cruel waters, she, death's agony o'er,
Must, in the washing of perennial waves,
In some far century, æons remote,
But in an hour sure-fixed of pitiful fate,
All-conscious still of love, despite the deep,

Float over some stray bone, some particle,
An all-diffused sense would know as his;
Then would she sit her down, and watch the tide,
Slow growing, till it touched at length her feet,
When, terror-stricken, she would spring upright,
And turn, and flee aghast, with white-rimmed eye.
　But still, where'er she fled, the strange voice followed;
Whisperings innumerable of water-drops
Growing together to a giant cry;
Which, now in hoarse, half-stifled undertone,
And now in thunderous peals of billowy shouts,
Called after her to come, and make no stay.
From the low mists that mingled with the clouds,
And from the tossings of the lifted waves,
Where plunged and rose the raving wilderness,
Voices, pursuing arms, and beckoning hands
Came shorewards, feeling, reaching after her.

Then would she fling her gaunt wild arms on high,
Over her head, in tossings like the waves,
Or fix them, with clasped hands of prayer intense,
Forward, appealing to the bitter sea;
Or sudden from her shoulders she would tear
Her garments, one by one, and cast them out
Into the roarings of the heedless surge,
A vain oblation to the hungry waves.
As vain was pity's care to cover her;
Best gifts but bribed the sea, and left her bare.
But such a fire was burning in her brain,
That all-unheeded, cold winds lapped her round,
And sleet-like spray flashed on her tawny skin.
Even her food she brought and flung it far,
To feed the sea—with naked arms, and hair
Streaming like rooted weed on windy tides,
Coal-black and lustreless. But evermore

Back came the wave, while floated yet at hand
Her sacrifice accepted; so despair,
Back surging, on her heart rushed ever afresh:
She sickening moaned—half-muttered and half-
	moaned—
"She will not be content; she'll have me yet."

   But when the night grew thick upon the sea,
Quenching it all, except its quenchless voice,
She, half-released until the light, would rise,
And step by step withdraw; as dreaming man,
With an eternity of slowness, drags
His earth-bound, lead-like, irresponsive feet
Back from a sleeping horror that will wake;
Until, upon the narrow beach arrived,
She turned her back at last upon her foe;
Then, clothed in all the might of the Unseen,
Terror grew ghastly, and she shrieked and fled—
Fled to the battered base of the old tower,
And round the rock, and through the arched gap,

Into the opening blackness of the vault,
And sank upon the sand, and gasped, and raved.
There, cowering in a nook, she sat all night,
Her eyes fixed on the entrance of the cave,
Through which a pale light shimmered—from the
    eye
Of the great sleepless ocean—Argus more dread
Than he with hundred lidless watching orbs;
And when she slept, still saw the sea in dreams.
But in the stormy nights, when all was dark,
And the wild tempest swept with slanting wing
Against her refuge; and the heavy spray
Shot through the doorway serpentine cold arms
To seize the fore-doomed morsel of the sea,
She slept not, evermore stung to new life
By new sea-terrors. Now it was the gull,
Whose clanging pinions darted through the arch,
And flapped about her head; and now a wave
Grown arrogant, that rushed into her vault,

Clasped her waist-high, and out again and away
To swell the devilish laughter in the fog :
It left her clinging to the rocky wall,
Watching with white face lest it came again ;
And though the tide were ebbing, she slept not yet,
But sat unmoving, till the low gray dawn
Grew on the misty dance of spouting waves,
Seen like a picture through the arched door ;
At which the old fascination woke and drew,
And, rising slowly, forth she went once more,
To haunt the border of the dawning sea.

  Yet all the time there lay within her soul
An inner chamber, quietest place : her love
Had closed its door, and held her in the storm.
She, entering there, had found a refuge calm
As summer evening, or a mother's arms.
There had she found her lost love, only lost
In that he slept nor yet would be awaked ;

And waiting for her there, watching the lost,
The Love that waits and watches evermore.

   Thou too hast such a chamber, quietest place,
Where God is waiting for thee. What is it
That will not let thee enter? Is it care
For the provision of the unborn day,
As if thou wert a God that must foresee?
Is it thy craving for the praise of men?
Ambition to outstrip them in the race
Of wealth or honour? Is it love of self,
The greed that still to have must still destroy?—
Go mad for some lost love; some voice of old,
Which first thou madest sing, and after sob;
Some heart thou foundest rich, and leftest bare,
Choking its well of faith with thy false deeds;
Not like thy God, who keeps the better wine
Until the last, and, if he giveth grief,
Giveth it first, and ends the tale with joy.
Such madness clings about the feet of God,

For love informs it. Better a thousandfold
Be she than thou! for though thy brain be strong
And clear and active, hers a withered fruit
That nourishes no seed; her heart is full
Of that in whose might God did make the
    world—
A living well, and thine an empty cup.
It was the invisible unbroken cord
Between the twain, her and her sailor-lad,
That drew her ever to the ocean marge.
Better to die, better to rave for love,
Than never to have loved; or having sought
The love of love, nor gained responsive boon,
To turn away with sickly sneering heart!
  But if thy heart be noble, think and say
If thou rememberest not one hour of torture,
When, maddened with the thought that could not
    be,
Thou mightst have yielded to the demon wind

That swept in tempest through thy scorching brain,
And rushed into the night, and howled aloud,
And clamoured to the waves, and beat the rocks;
And never found thy way back to the seat
Of conscious self, and power to rule thy pain,
Had not God made thee strong to bear and live;
Then own at least this woman's story fit
For poet's tale; and in her wildest moods,
Acknowledge her thy sister.   Then thy love,
In the sad face, whose eyes, like suns too fierce,
Have parched and paled the cheeks—in that spare
    form,
Deformed by tempests of the soul and sea,
Will soon unmask a shape of loveliness
Fit to remind thee of a story old
Which God has in his keeping—of thyself.

  But not forgot are children when they sleep
The darkness lasts all night and clears the eyes;
Then comes the morning and the joy of light.

O surely madness hideth not from Him!
Nor doth a soul cease to be beautiful
In his sight, that its beauty is withdrawn,
And hid by pale eclipse from human eyes.
As the white snow is friendly to the earth,
And pain and loss are friendly to the soul,
Shielding it from the black heart-killing frost;
So may a madness be one of God's winters,
And when the winter over is and gone,
Then smile the skies, and blooms the earth again.
For the fair time of singing birds is come:
Into the cold wind and the howling night,
God sent for her, and she was carried in
Where there was no more sea.

      What messenger
Ran from the door of heaven to bring her home?
The sea, her terror.

      In the rocks that stand
Below the cliff, there lies a rounded hollow,

Scooped like a basin, with jagged and pinnacled
    sides:
This, buried low when winds heap up the tide,
Lifts in the respiration of the surge,
Its broken, toothed edge, and deep within,
Lies resting water, radiantly clear.
There, on a morn of sunshine, while the wind
Yet blew, and heaved yet the billowy sea
With memories of a night of stormy dreams,
At rest they found her: in the sleep which is
And is not death, she, lying very still,
Gathered the bliss that follows after pain.
O life of love, conquered at last by fate!
O life raised from the dead by saviour Death!
O love unconquered and invincible!
The enemy sea had cooled her burning brain;
Had laid to rest those limbs that could not rest;
Had hid the horror of its own dread face.
'Twas but one desolate cry, and then her fear

Became a blessed fact, and straight she knew
What God knew all the time, that it was well.

  O thou whose feet tread ever the wet sands
And howling rocks along the wearing shore,
Roaming the confines of the sea of death!
Strain not thine eyes, bedimmed with longing tears;
No sail comes climbing back across that line.
Turn thee and to thy work; let God alone;
And wait for him: faint o'er the waves will come
Far floating whispers from the other shore
To thine averted ears. Do thou thy work,
And thou shalt follow; follow, and find thine own.

  And thou who fearest something that may come!
Around whose house the storm of terror breaks
All night! to whose love-sharpened ear, all day,
The Invisible is calling at the door,

To render up a life thou canst not keep,
Or love that will not stay!—open thy door,
And carry forth thy dying to the marge
Of the great sea; yea, walk into the flood,
And lay the bier upon the moaning waves.
Give God thy dead to bury; float it again,
With sighs and prayers to waft it through the
    gloom,
Back to the spring of life. Say—"If it die,
Yet thou, the life of life, art still alive,
And thou canst make thy dead alive again."

  Ah God! the earth is full of cries and moans,
And dull despair, that neither moans nor cries;
Thousands of hearts are waiting helplessly;
The whole creation groaneth, travaileth
For what it knows not, but with dull-eyed hope
Of resurrection, or of dreamless death!
Raise thou the dead of Aprils past and gone
In hearts of maidens; restore the autumn fruits

Of old men feebly mournful o'er the life
Which scarce hath memory but the mournfulness.
There is no past with thee: bring back once more
The summer eves of lovers, over which
The wintry wind that raveth through the world
Heaps wretched leaves, half tombed in ghastly snow;
Bring back the mother-heaven of orphans lone,
The brother's and the sister's faithfulness;
Bring forth the kingdom of the Son of Man.

   They troop around me, children wildly crying;
Women with faded eyes, all spent of tears;
Men who have lived for love, yet lived alone;
And other worse, whose grief cannot be said.
O God, thou hast a work fit for thy strength,
To save these hearts of thine with full content—
Except thou give them Lethe's stream to drink,
And that, my God, were all unworthy thee.

Dome up, O heaven! yet higher o'er my head;
Back, back, horizon! widen out my world;
Rush in, O infinite sea of the Unknown!
For, though he slay me, I will trust in **God.**

TO LADY NOEL BYRON.

They sought and sought, for wealth's dear sake,
  The wizard men of old,
After the secret that should make
  The meaner metals gold.

A nobler alchymy is thine,
  Learned in thy sore distress:
Gold in thy hand becomes divine—
  Grows truth and tenderness.

TO THE SAME.

Dead, why defend thee, who in life
   Would'st for thy foe have died?
Who, thy own name the word of strife,
   Hadst silent stood aside.

Grand in forgiveness, what to thee
   The moralizer's prate?
Or thy great heart hath ceased to be,
   Or loveth still its mate.

TO AURELIO SAFFI.

To God and man be simply true;
Do as thou hast been wont to do;
Or, *Of the old more in the new,*
Mean all the same when said to you.

I love thee: thou art calm and strong,
Firm in the right, mild to the wrong;
Thy heart, in every raging throng,
A chamber shut for prayer and song.

Defeat thou know'st not, canst not know;
'Tis that thy aims so lofty go,
They need as long to root and grow
As infant hills to reach the snow.

TO AURELIO SAFFI.

Press on and prosper, holy friend.
I, weak and ignorant, would lend
A voice, thee, strong and wise, to send
Prospering onward, without end.

THE DISCIPLE.

THE DISCIPLE.

I.

THE times are changed, and gone the day
   When the high heavenly land,
Though unbeheld, quite near them lay,
   And men could understand.

The dead yet find it, who, when here,
   Did love it more than this;
They enter in, are filled with cheer,
   And pain expires in bliss.

All-glorious gleams the blessed land
   Ah God ! I weep and pray :
The heart thou holdest in thy hand
   Loves more this sunny day.

I see the hundred thousand wait
   Around the radiant throne :
Ah, what a dreary, gilded state !
   What crowds of beings lone !

I do not care for singing psalms ;
   I tire of good men's talk ;
To me there is no joy in palms,
   Or white-robed, solemn walk.

I love to hear the wild winds meet,
   The wild old winds at night ;
To watch the cold stars flash and beat,
   The feathery snow alight.

I love all tales of valiant men,
    Of women good and fair :
If I were rich and strong, ah ! then
    I would do something rare.

But for thy temple in the sky,
    Its pillars strong and white—
I cannot love it, though I try,
    And long with all my might.

Sometimes a joy lays hold on me,
    And I am speechless then ;
Almost a martyr I could be,
    To join the holy men.

Straightway my heart is like a clod,
    My spirit wrapt in doubt :
" A pillar in the house of God,
    And never more go out !"

No more the sunny, breezy morn ;
    No more the glowing noon ;
No more the silent heath forlorn ;
    No more the waning moon !

My God, this heart will never burn,
    Will never taste thy joy ;
Even Jesus' face is calm and stern:
    I am a hapless boy.

*   *   *   *

ii.

I READ good books. My heart despairs.
    In vain I try to dress
My soul in feelings like to theirs—
    These men of holiness.

My thoughts, like doves, abroad I fling
  To find a country fair :
Wind-baffled, back, they, with tired wing,
  To my poor ark repair.

Or comes a sympathetic thrill
  With long-departed saint,
A feeble dawn, without my will,
  Of feelings old and quaint,

As of a church's holy night,
  With low-browed chapels round,
Where common sunshine dares not light
  On the too sacred ground,—

One glance at sunny fields of grain,
  One shout of child at play—
A merry melody drives amain
  The one-toned chant away.

My spirit will not enter here,
    To haunt the holy gloom ;
I gaze into a mirror mere,
    A mirror, not a room.

And as a bird against the pane
    Oft strikes, deceived sore,
So I, who would go in, remain
    Outside some closed door.

Oh ! it will cost me many a sigh,
    If this be what it claims—
This book, so unlike earth and sky,
    Unlike my hopes and aims ;

To me a desert parched and bare,
    In which a spirit broods
Whose wisdom I would gladly share
    At cost of many goods.

   *   *   *   *

THE DISCIPLE.

III.

O HEAR me, God! O give me joy,
    Such as thy chosen feel;
Have pity on a wretched boy,
    Whose heart is hard as steel.

I have no care for what is good;
    Thyself I do not love;
I relish not this bible-food;
    My heaven is not above.

Thou wilt not hear. I come no more.
    Thou heedest not my woe.
With sighs and tears my heart is sore.
    Thou comest not. I go.

IV.

Once more I kneel. The earth is dark,
    And darker yet the air;
If light there be, 'tis but a spark
    Amid a world's despair—

A hopeless hope there yet may be
    A God somewhere to hear;
A God to whom I bend my knee,
    A God with open ear.

I know that men laugh still to scorn
    The grief that is my lot;
Such wounds, they say, are hardly borne,
    But easily forgot.

What matter that my sorrows rest
   On ills which men despise !
More hopeless heaves my aching breast,
   Than when a prophet sighs.

Æons of griefs have come and gone—
   My grief is yet my mark.
The sun sets every night, yet none
   Sees therefore in the dark.

There's love enough upon the earth,
   And beauty too, they say :
There may be plenty, may be dearth,
   I care not any way.

The world has melted from my sight ;
   No grace in life is left ;
I cry to thee with all my might,
   Because I am bereft.

In vain I cry. The earth is dark,
   And darker yet the air;
Of light there trembles now no spark
   In my lost soul's despair.

*   *   *   *

V.

I SIT and gaze from window high
   Down on the noisy street.
No part in this great coil have I,
   No fate to go and meet.

My books unopened long have lain;
   In class I am all astray:
The questions growing in my brain,
   Demand and have their way.

Knowledge is power, the people cry;
  Grave men the lure repeat:
After some rarer thing I sigh,
  That makes the pulses beat.

Old truths, new facts, they preach aloud—
  Their tones like wisdom fall:
One sunbeam glancing on a cloud,
  Hints things beyond them all.

*   *   *   *

VI.

But something is not right within;
  High hopes are all gone by.
Was it a bootless aim—to win
  Sight of a loftier sky?

They preach men should not faint, but pray,
   And seek until they find ;
But God is very far away,
   Nor is his countenance kind.

And yet I know my father prayed,
   Withdrawing from the throng ;
I think some answer must have made
   His heart so high and strong.

Once more I'll seek the God of men,
   Redeeming childhood's vow.
—I failed with bitter weeping then,
   And fail cold-hearted now

VII.

Why search for God? A man I tread
   This old life-bearing earth;
High thoughts arise and lift my head—
   In me they have their birth.

The preacher says a Christian must
   Do all the good he can;
I must be noble, true, and just,
   Because I am a man.

They say a man must wake, and keep
   Lamp burning, garments white,
Else he shall sit without and weep
   When Christ comes home at night;

I say, his manhood must be free;
   Himself he dares not stain;
He must not soil the dignity
   Of heart and blood and brain.

Yes, I say well! for words are cheap.
   What action have I borne?
What praise will my one talent reap?
   What grapes are on my thorn?

Have high words kept me pure enough?
   In evil have I no part?
Hath not my bosom "perilous stuff,
   That weighs upon the heart"?

I am not that I well may praise;
   I do not that I say;
I sit a talker in the ways,
   A dreamer in the day.

VIII

The preacher's words are true, I know,
    That man may lose his life;
That every man must downward go
    Without the upward strife.

'Twere well my soul should cease to roam,
    Should seek and have and hold
It may be there is yet a home
    In that religion old.

Again I kneel, again I pray·
    Wilt thou be God to me?
Wilt thou give ear to what I say,
    And lift me up to thee?

Lord, is it true? Oh, vision high!
   The clouds of heaven dispart;
An opening depth of loving sky
   Looks down into my heart.

There *is* a home wherein to dwell—
   The very heart of light!
Thyself my sun immutable,
   My moon and stars all night!

I thank thee, Lord. It must be so,
   Its beauty is so good.
Up in my heart thou mad'st it go,
   And I have understood.

The clouds return. The common day
   Falls on me like a *No;*
But I have seen what might be—may;
   And with a hope I go.

IX.

I AM a stranger in the land,
    It gives no welcome dear;
The lilies bloom not for my hand,
    The roses for my cheer.

The sunshine used to make me glad,
    But now it knows me not;
This weight of brightness makes me sad —
    It isolates a blot.

I am forgotten by the hills,
    And by the river's play;
No look of recognition thrills
    The features of the day.

Then only am I moved to song,
    When down the darkening street,
While vanishes the scattered throng,
    The driving rain I meet.

The rain pours down. My thoughts awake,
    Like flowers that languished long.
From bare cold hills the night-winds break,
    From me the unwonted song.

X.

I READ the Bible with my eyes,
    But hardly with my brain;
Should this the meaning recognize,
    My heart yet reads in vain.

These words of promise and of woe
    Seem but a tinkling sound;
As through an ancient tomb I go,
    With dust-filled urns around.

Or, as a sadly searching child,
    Afar from love and home,
Sits in an ancient chamber piled
    With scroll and musty tome;

So I, in these epistles old
    From men of heavenly care,
Find all the thoughts of other mould
    Than I can love or share.

No sympathy with mine they show,
    Their world is not the same;
They move me not with joy or woe,
    They touch me not with blame.

I hear no word that calls my life,
   Or owns my struggling powers;
Those ancient ages had their strife,
   But not a strife like ours.

Oh! not like men they move and speak,
   Those pictures in old panes;
Nor alter they their aspect meek
   For all the winds and rains.

Their thoughts are filled with figures strange
   Of Jewish forms and rites:
A world of air and sea I range,
   Of mornings and of nights.

XI.

I TURN me to the gospel-tale.
   My hope is faint with fear
That neediest search will not avail
   To find a refuge here.

A misty wind blows bare and rude
   From the dead sea of the past;
And through the clouds that halt and brood,
   Dim dawns a shape at last:

A sad worn man who bows his face,
   And treads a frightful path,
To save an abject hopeless race
   From an eternal wrath.

Kind words he speaks—but all the time
   As from a pathless height
Where human feet can never climb,
   Half-swathed in ancient night.

And sometimes, to a gentle heart,
   His words unkindly flow;
Surely it is no Saviour's part
   To speak to women so.

Much rather would I refuge take
   With Mary, dear to me,
To whom those rough hard words he spake,
   What have I to do with thee?

Surely I know men tenderer,
   Women of larger soul,
Who need no prayers their hearts to stir,
   Who always would make whole.

THE DISCIPLE.

Oftenest he looks a weary saint,
    Embalmed in pallid gleam,
Listless and sad, without complaint,
    Like dead man in a dream.

But at the best he is uplift
    A spectacle, a show :
To me, an old, an outworn gift,
    Whose worth I cannot know.

I have no love to pay my debt—
    He leads me from the sun.
Yet it is hard men should forget
    The kindness he has done ;

That he, to expiate a curse,
    Upon that altar-hill,
Beneath a sunless universe,
    Did suffer, patient, still

But what is he, whose pardon slow
    At so much blood is priced?—
If such thou art, O Jove, I go
    To the Promethean Christ.

XII.

A WORD within says I am to blame,
    And therefore must confess;
Must call my doing by its name,
    And so make evil less.

"I could not his false triumph bear,
    For he was first in wrong."
Thy own ill-doings are thy care,
    His to himself belong."

"To do it right, my heart should own
  Some sorrow for the ill."
" Plain, honest words will half atone,
  And they are in thy will."

The struggle comes. Evil or I
  Must gain the victory now.
I am unmoved, and yet would try :
  O God, to thee I bow.

The skies are brass; there falls no aid;
  No wind of help will blow.
But I bethink me :—I am made
  A man : I rise and go.

XIII.

To Christ I needs must come, they say,
    Who went to death for me:
I turn aside; I come, I pray,
    My unknown God, to thee.

He is afar; the story old
    Is blotted, worn, and dim;
With thee, O God, I can be bold—
    I cannot pray to him.

Pray! At the word a cloudy grief
    Around me folds its pall:
With nothing to be called belief,
    How can I pray at all?

THE DISCIPLE.

I know not if a God be there
    To heed my crying sore,
If in the great world anywhere
    An ear keep open door.

An unborn faith I will not nurse;
    Nor search—an endless task;
But loud into its universe
    My soul shall call and ask.

Is there no God—earth, sky, and sea
    Are but a chaos wild;
Is there a God—I know that he
    Must hear his calling child.

THE DISCIPLE.

XIV.

I KNEEL. But all my soul is dumb
    With hopeless misery:
Is *he* a friend who will not come,
    Whose face I may not see?

It is not fear of broken laws,
    Or judge's damning word;
It is a lonely pain, because
    I call and am not heard.

A cry where no man is to hear,
    Doubles the lonely pain;
Returns in silence on the ear,
    In torture on the brain.

No look of love a smile can bring,
  No kiss wile back the breath
To cold lips : I no answer wring
  From this great face of death.

XV.

YET sometimes when the agony
  Dies of its own excess,
Unhoped repose descends on me,
  A rain of gentleness ;

A sense of bounty and of grace,
  A calm within my breast,
As if the shadow of His face
  Did fall on me and rest.

'Tis God, I say, and cry no more—
    Upraised, with strength to stand
And wait unwearied at the door,
    Till comes an opening hand.

XVI.

BUT is it God?—Once more the fear
    Of *No God* loads my breath:
Amidst a sunless atmosphere,
    I rise to fight with death.

This rest may be but such as lulls
    The man who fainting lies:
His bloodless brain his spirit dulls,
    With darkness veils his eyes.

THE DISCIPLE.

But even this, my heart responds,
   May be the ancient rest
Rising released from frozen bonds
   To flow and fill the breast.

The o'ertasked will falls down aghast,
   In individual death;
Then God takes up the severed past,
   And breathes the primal breath.

For torture's self can breed no calm,
   Nor death to life give birth;
No labour can create the balm
   That soothes the sleeping earth.

So I will hope it is The One
   Whose peace is life in me,
Who, when my strength is overdone,
   Inspires serenity.

XVII.

When the hot sun's too urgent might
    Hath shrunk the tender leaf,
The dew slides down the blessed night,
    And cools its fainting grief.

When poet's heart is in eclipse,
    A glance from childhood's eye,
A smile from passing maiden's lips,
    Will clear a glowing sky.

Might not from God such influence come
    A dying hope to lift?
Could he not send, in trouble, some
    Unmediated gift?

My child is moaning. Far in dreams
   Which her own heart has made,
A world no caring love redeems
   She wanders, much afraid.

I lay my hand upon her breast;
   Her moaning dies away;
She waketh not; but, lost in rest,
   Sleeps on into the day.

And when my heart with soft release
   Grows calm as summer-sea,
Shall I not hope the God of peace
   Hath laid his hand on me?

THE DISCIPLE.

XVIII.

But why from thought should fresh doubt start—
   An ever-lengthening cord ?
Might he not make my troubled heart
   Right sure it was the Lord ?

God will not give a little boon
   To turn thee from the best ;
A granted sign might all too soon
   Rejoice thee into rest.

Yet could not any sign, though grand
   As hosts of fire about,
Though lovely as a sunset-land,
   Secure thy soul from doubt.

THE DISCIPLE.

A smile from one thou lovest well
   May glad thee all the day;
All day afar thy doubt may dwell—
   Return with twilight gray.

For doubt will come, will ever come,
   Though signs be perfect good,
Till face to face strikes doubting dumb,
   And both are understood.

XIX.

I shall behold him, one day, nigh.
   Assailed with glory keen,
My eyes shall open wide, and I
   Shall see as I am seen.

Of nothing can my heart be sure
    Except the highest, best :
When God I see with vision pure,
    That sight will be my rest.

Therefore I look with longing eye,
    And still my hope renew ;
Still think that comfort from the sky
    May come like falling dew.

XX.

But if a vision should unfold
    That I might banish fear ;
That I, the chosen, might be bold,
    And walk with upright cheer,

My heart would cry: But shares my race
   In this great love of thine?
I pray, put me not in good case,
   If others lack and pine.

Nor claim I thus a loving heart
   That for itself is mute:
In such love I desire no part
   As reaches not my root.

If all my brothers thou dost call
   As children to thy knee,
Thou givest me my being's all,
   Thou sayest *child* to me.

If thou to me alone shouldst give,
   My heart were all beguiled:
It would not be *because* I live,
   And am my Father's child.

XXI.

As little comfort would it bring,
    Amidst a throng to pass;
To stand with thousands worshipping
    Upon the sea of glass;

To know that, of a sinful world,
    I one was saved as well;
My roll of ill with theirs upfurled,
    And cast in deepest hell;

That God looked bounteously on one,
    Because on many men;
As shone Judea's earthly sun
    Upon the healed ten.

No; thou must be a God to me
    As if but me were none;
I such a perfect child to thee
    As if thou hadst but one.

XXII.

Then, O my Father, hast thou not
    A blessing even for me?
Shall I be, barely, not forgot?
    Never come home to thee?

Hast thou no care for this one child,
    This thinking, living need?
Or is thy countenance only mild,
    Thy heart not love indeed?

For some eternal joy I pray,
   To make me strong and free;
Yea, such a friend I need alway
   As thou alone canst be.

Art thou not, by infinitude,
   Able, in every man,
To turn thyself to every mood
   Since ever life began?

Art thou not each man's God—his own,
   With secret words between,
As thou and he lived all alone,
   Insphered in silence keen?

Ah God! my heart is not the same
   As any heart beside;
Nor is my sorrow or my blame,
   My tenderness or pride.

My story too, thou knowest, God,
   Is different from the rest;
Thou knowest—none but thee—the load
   With which my heart is pressed.

Hence I to thee a love might bring,
   By none besides me due;
One praiseful song at least might sing
   Which could not but be new.

XXIII.

Nor seek I thus to stand apart
   In thee, my kind above;
'Tis only that my aching heart
   Must rest ere it can love.

If thou love not, I have no care,
    No power to love, no hope.
What is life here or anywhere?
    Or why with darkness cope?

I scorn love's every motion, sign,
    So feeble, selfish, low,
If thy love give no pledge that mine
    Shall one day perfect grow.

But if thy love were only such,
    As, tender and intense,
As, tested by its human touch,
    Would satisfy my sense

Of what a father never was
    But should be to his son,
My heart would leap for joy, because
    My rescue was begun.

And then my love, by thine set free,
  Would overflow thy men;
In every face my heart would see
  God shining out again.

There are who hold high festival. .
  And at the board crown Death:
I am too weak to live at all, . .
  Except I breathe thy breath.

Show me a love that nothing bates,
  Absolute, self-severe,
And at Gehenna's prayerless gates
  "I cannot taint with fear."

THE DISCIPLE.

XXIV.

I CANNOT brook that men should say—
    Nor this for gospel take—
That thou wilt hear me if I pray
    Asking for Jesus' sake.

For love to him is not to me,
    And cannot lift my fate;
The love is not that is not free,
    Perfect, immediate.

Love is salvation: life without
    No moment can endure.
Those sheep alone go in and out,
    Who know thy love is pure.

THE DISCIPLE.

XXV.

But what if God requires indeed,
   For cause yet unrevealed,
Assent to moulded form of creed,
   Such as I cannot yield?

The words may have some other sense,
   Or we be different
From what we seem when thought intense
   Is only one way bent.

Or God may choose to give a test,
    And try the earnest aim,
That only he may win the best,
    Who conquers pride and shame.

And yet the words I cannot say
    With the responding folk;
I at his feet a heart would lay,
    Not shoulders for the yoke.

"And wilt thou bargain then with Him?"
    Some priest will make reply.
I answer: "Though the sky be dim,
    My hope is in the sky."

XXVI.

But is my will alive, awake?
    The one God will not heed,
If in my lips or hands I take
    A half-word or half-deed.

Day after day I sit and dream,
    Amazed in outwardness;
The powers of things that only seem
    The things that are oppress.

Till in my soul some discord sounds,
    Till sinks some yawning lack
. turn me from life's rippling rounds,
    And unto thee come back.

Thou seest how poor a thing am I;
   Yet hear, whate'er I be;
Despairing of my will, I cry,
   Be God enough to me.

My being low, irresolute,
   I cast before thy feet;
And wait, while even prayer is mute,
   For what thou judgest meet.

XXVII.

My safety lies not, any hour,
   In what I generate,
But in the living, healing power
   Of that which doth create.

THE DISCIPLE.

If he is God to the incomplete,
    Fulfilling lack and need,
Then I *may* cast before his feet
    A half-word or half-deed.

I bring, Lord, to thy altar-stair,
    To thee, love-glorious,
My very lack of will and prayer,
    Crying, Thou seest me thus.

From some old well of life they flow
    The words my being fill !—
" Of me that man the truth shall know
    Who wills the Father's will."

XXVIII.

What is his will?—that I may go
   And do it in the hope
That light will rise and spread and grow,
   As deed enlarges scope.

I need not search the sacred book
   To find my duty clear;
Scarce in my bosom need I look,
   It lies so very near.

Henceforward I must watch the door
   Of word and action too;
There's one thing I must do no more,
   Another I must do.

THE DISCIPLE.

Alas, these are such little things!
    No glory in their birth!
Doubt from their common aspect springs,
    If God will count them worth.

But here I am not left to choose,
    My duty is my lot;
And weighty things will glory lose,
    If small ones are forgot.

I am not worthy high things yet;
    I'll humbly do my own;
Good care of sheep may so beget
    A fitness for the throne.

Ah fool! why dost thou reason thus?
    Ambition's very fool!
Through high and low, each glorious,
    Shines God's all-perfect rule.

'Tis God I need, not rank in good;
  'Tis Life, not honour's meed;
With him to fill my every mood,
  I am content indeed.

XXIX.

Will do: shall know: I feel the force,
  The fulness of the word;
His holy boldness held its course,
  Claiming divine accord.

What if, as yet, I have never seen
  The true face of the Man?
The named notion may have been
  A likeness vague and wan;

THE DISCIPLE.

Or bright with such unblended hues
    As on his chamber wall
The humble peasant gladly views,
    And Jesus Christ doth call.

The story I did never scan
    With vision calm and strong;
Have never tried to see the Man,
    The many words among

Some faces that would never please
    With any sweet surprise,
Gain on the heart by slow degrees
    Until they feast the eyes;

And if I ponder, day by day,
    Over the storied place,
Through mists that slowly melt away
    May dawn a human face.

A face! What face? Exalting thought
    That face may dawn on me
Which Moses on the mountain sought,
    God would not let him see.

XXX.

I READ and read the ancient tale,
    A gracious form I mark;
But dim and faint as wrapt in veil
    Of Sinai's cloudy dark.

I see a simple, truthful man,
    Who walks the earth erect,
Nor stoops his noble head to one
    From fear or false respect.

He seeks to climb no high estate,
    No low consent secure,
With high and low serenely great,
    Because his ends are pure;

Nor walks alone, beyond our reach,
    Our joy and grief beyond:
He counts it joy divine to teach,
    When human hearts respond;

And grief divine oft woke in him
    O'er souls that lay and slept:
"How often, O Jerusalem!"
    He said, and gazed, and wept.

Hid in his heart, some spring of grace
    Flowed silent through the din;
The sorrow-cloud upon his face,
    Was lighted from within.

Love was his very being's root,
   And healing was its flower;
Love only, root and flower and fruit—
   Beginning, end, and power.

O Life of Jesus—the unseen,
   Which found such glorious show—
Deeper than death, and more serene!
   How poor am I! how low!

XXXI.

As in a living well I gaze,
  Kneeling upon its brink.
What are the very words he says?
  What did the one man think?

I find his heart was all above;
  Obedience his one thought;
Reposing in his father's love,
  His will alone he sought.

  * * * *

XXXII.

Years have passed o'er my broken plan
    To picture out a strife,
Where ancient Death, in horror wan,
    Faced young and fearing Life.

More of the tale I tell not so—
    But for myself would say:
My heart is quiet with what I know,
    With what I hope, is gay.

And where I cannot set my faith,
    Unknowing or unwise,
I say "If this be what *he* saith,
    Here hidden treasure lies."

Through years gone by since thus I strove,
   Thus shadowed out my strife,
While at my history I wove,
   Thou didst weave in the life.

Through poverty that had no lack,
   For friends divinely good;
Through pain that not too long did rack
   Through love that understood;

Through light that taught me what to hold,
   And what to cast away;
Through thy forgiveness manifold,
   And things I cannot say,

Here thou hast brought me—able now
   To kiss thy garment's hem,
Entirely to thy will to bow,
   And trust thee even for them.

THE DISCIPLE.

Who, lost in darkness, in the mire,
    With ill-contented feet,
Walk trailing loose their white attire,
    For the sapphire-floor unmeet.

Lord Jesus Christ, I know not how —
    With this blue air, blue sea,
This yellow sand, that grassy brow,
    All isolating me—

My words to thy heart should draw near,
    My thoughts be heard by thee
But he who made the ear must hear,
    Who made the eye, must see.

Thou mad'st the hand with which I write,
    That sun descending slow
Through rosy gates, that purple light
    On waves that shoreward go,

THE DISCIPLE.

Bowing their heads in golden spray,
    As if thy foot were near :
I think I know thee, Lord, to-day,
    Have known thee many a year.

I know thy Father—thine and mine—
    Thus thy great word doth go :
If thy great word the words combine,
    I will not say *Not so*.

Lord, thou hast much to make me yet—
    A feeble infant still :
Thy thoughts, Lord, in my bosom set,
    Fulfil me of thy will,

Even of thy truth, both in and out,
    That so I question free :
The man that feareth, Lord, to doubt,
    In that fear doubteth thee.

THE GOSPEL WOMEN.

THE GOSPEL WOMEN.

I.

THE MOTHER MARY.

1.

MARY, to thee the heart was given
    For infant hand to hold,
Thus clasping, an eternal heaven,
    The great earth in its fold.

He seized the world with tender might
    By making thee his own;
Thee, lowly queen, whose heavenly height
    Was to thyself unknown.

He came, all helpless, to thy power,
    For warmth, and love, and birth;
In thy embraces, every hour,
    He grew into the earth.

And thine the grief, O mother high,
    Which all thy sisters share,
Who keep the gate betwixt the sky
    And this our lower air;

And unshared sorrows, gathering slow;
    New thoughts within thy heart,
Which through thee like a sword will go,
    And make thee mourn apart.

For, if a woman bore a son
    That was of angel brood,
Who lifted wings ere day was done,
    And soared from where he stood;

Strange grief would fill each mother-moan,
    Wild longing, dim, and sore :
"My child ! my child ! he is my own,
    And yet is mine no more ! "

So thou, O Mary, years on years,
    From child-birth to the cross,
Wast filled with yearnings, filled with fears,
    Keen sense of love and loss.

His childish thoughts outsoared thy reach ;
    Even his tenderness
Had deeper springs than act or speech
    Could unto thee express.

Strange pangs await thee, mother mild !
    A sorer travail-pain,
Before the spirit of thy child
    Is born in thee again.

And thou wilt still forebode and dread,
    And loss be still thy fear,
Till form be gone, and, in its stead,
    The very self appear.

For, when thy son hath reached his goal,
    And vanished from the earth,
Soon shalt thou find him in thy soul,
    A second, holier birth.

2.

AH, there he stands! With wondering face
  Old men surround the boy;
The solemn looks, the awful place
  Bestill the mother's joy.

In sweet reproach her joy is hid;
  Her trembling voice is low,
Less like the chiding than the chid:
  "How couldst thou leave us so?"

But will her dear heart understand
  The answer that he gives—
Childlike, eternal, simple, grand,
  The law by which he lives?

"Why sought ye me?" Ah, mother dear!
   The gulf already opes
That soon will keep thee to thy fear,
   And part thee from thy hopes.

"My Father's business—that ye know,
   I cannot choose but do."
Mother, if he that work forego,
   Not long he cares for you.

Creation's harder, better part
   Is in his willing hand;
marvel not the mother's heart
   Not yet could understand.

3.

The Lord of life among them rests;
    They quaff the merry wine;
They do not know, those wedding guests,
    The present power divine.

Believe, on such a group he smiled,
    Though he might sigh the while;
Believe not, sweet-souled Mary's child
    Was born without a smile.

He saw the pitchers high upturned,
    The last red drops to pour;
His mother's cheek with triumph burned,
    And expectation wore.

He knew the prayer her bosom housed,
    He read it in her eyes;
Her hopes in him sad thoughts have roused
    Before her words arise.

"They have no wine," her shy lips said,
    With prayer but half-begun;
Her eyes went on, "Lift up thy head,
    Show what thou art, my son!"

A vision rose before his eyes,
    The cross, the waiting tomb,
The people's rage, the darkened skies,
    His unavoided doom.

"Ah woman-heart! what end is set
    Common to thee and me?
My hour of honour is not yet,—
    'T will come too soon for thee."

The word was dark ; the tone was kind ;
   His heart the mother knew ;
And still his eyes more sweetly shined,
   His voice more gentle grew.

Another, on the word intent,
   Had heard refusal there ;
His mother heard a full consent,
   A sweetly answered prayer.

"Whate'er he saith unto you, do."
   Fast flowed the grapes divine ;
Though then, as now, not many knew
   Who made the water wine.

4.

"He is beside himself." Dismayed,
   His mother, brothers talked:
"He from the well-known path has strayed,
   In which our fathers walked."

And sad at heart, they sought him. Loud
   Some one the message bore:
He stands within, amidst a crowd,
   They at the open door.

"Thy mother and thy brothers would
   Speak with thee. Lo, they stand
Without and wait thee!" Like a flood
   Of sunrise on the land,

A new-born light his face o'erspread;
   Out from his eyes it poured;
He lifted up that gracious head,
   Looked round him, took the word:

"My mother—brothers—who are they?"
   Hearest thou, Mary mild?
This is a sword that well may slay—
   Disowned by thy child!

Ah, no! My brothers, sisters, hear!
   What says our humble lord?
O mother, did it wound *thy* ear?
   We thank him for the word.

"Who are my friends?" Oh! hear him say,
   Stretching his hand abroad:
"My mother, sisters, brothers, they
   Who do the will of God."

My brother! Lord of life and me,
    If it might come to this!
Ah! brother, sister, that would be
    Enough for all amiss.

Yea, hear him, mother, and rejoice:
    No better name hath he,
To give us best of all his choice,
    Than that he gives to thee.

O humble child, O faithful son!
    Of women most forlorn,
She who the Father's will hath done,
    The Son of Man hath borne.

Mary, if in thy coming pain,
    Thou to thy Father bow,
The Christ shall be thy son again,
    And twice his mother thou.

5.

Life's best things crowd around its close,
  To light it from the door;
When woman's aid no further goes,
  She weeps and loves the more.

Oft, oft, she doubted, in his life,
  And feared his mission's loss;
But now she shares the losing strife,
  And weeps beside the cross.

The dreaded hour is come at last;
  The sword has reached her soul;
The hour of timid hope is past,
  Unveiled the awful whole.

There hangs the son her body bore,
   Who in her arms did rest;
Those limbs the nails and hammer tore,
   Have lain upon her breast.

He speaks. With torturing joy the sounds
   Invade her desolate ear;
The mother's heart, though bleeding, bounds
   Her dying son to hear.

"Woman, behold thy son.—Behold
   Thy mother." Best relief—
That woful love in hers to fold
   Which next to hers was chief!

Another son, but not instead,
   He gave, lest grief should kill,
While he was down among the dead,
   Doing his Father's will.

No, not *instead*; the coming grace
  Shall make him hers anew—
More hers than when, in her embrace,
  His life from hers he drew.

II.

THE WOMAN THAT LIFTED UP HER VOICE.

FILLED with his words of truth and right,
 Her heart will break or cry :
A woman's cry bursts forth in might
 Of loving agony.

"Blessed the womb, thee, Lord, that bare !
 The bosom that thee fed !"
A moment's silence filled the air,
 When she the word had said.

He turns his face to meet the cry ;
 He knows from whence it springs—
A woman's heart that glad would die
 For woman's best of things.

THE WOMAN THAT CRIED ALOUD.

Such son to bear, such son to rear,
   The generations laud.
"Yea, rather, blessed they that hear
   And keep the word of God."

The tone was love and not rebuke;
   But, 'mid the murmured stir,
She, sure, was silent in her nook;
   No answer came from her.

III.

THE MOTHER OF ZEBEDEE'S CHILDREN.

SHE knelt, she bore a bold request,
   Though shy to speak it out;
Ambition, even in mother's breast,
   Before him stood in doubt.

"What is it?" "These my sons, allow
   To sit on thy right hand
And on thy left, O Lord, when thou
   Art ruler in the land."

"Ye know not what ye ask." There lay
   A baptism and a cup
They understood not, in the way
   By which he must go up.

She would have had them lifted high
  Above their fellow men;
Sharing their pride with mother-eye,
  Had been blest mother then.

But would she praise for granted quest,
  Counting her prayer well heard,
If of the three on Calvary's crest
  They shared the first and third?

She knoweth neither way nor end;
  There comes a dark despair,
When she will doubt if this great friend
  Can answer any prayer.

Yet higher than her love can dare,
  His love her sons will set:
They shall his cup and baptism share,
  And share his kingdom yet

They, entering at his palace-door,
    Shall shun the lofty seat;
Shall gird themselves, and water pour,
    And wash each other's feet.

For in thy kingdom, lowly Lord,
    Who sit with thee on high
Are those who tenderest help afford
    In most humility.

IV.

THE SYROPHENICIAN WOMAN.

"Grant, Lord, her prayer, and let her go;
   She crieth after us."
Nay, to the dogs ye cast it so;
   Serve not a woman thus.

Their pride, by condescension fed,
   He speaks with truer tongue·
"It is not meet the children's bread
   Should to the dogs be flung."

The words, because they were so sore,
   His tender voice did rue;
His face a gentle sadness wore,
   And showed he suffered too.

He makes her share the hurt of good,
   Takes what she would have lent,
That those proud men their evil mood
   May see, and so repent;

And that the hidden faith in her
   May burst in soaring flame,
From childhood deeper, holier,
   If birthright not the same.

"Truth, Lord; and yet the dogs that crawl
   Under the table, eat
The crumbs the little ones let fall—
   And that is not unmeet."

Ill names, of proud religion born—
   She'll wear the worst that comes;
Will clothe her, patient, in their scorn,
   To share the healing crumbs.

The cry rebuff could not abate
   Was not like water spilt :
"O woman, but thy faith is great !
   Be it even as thou wilt."

Oh, happy she who will not tire,
   But, baffled, prayeth still !
What if he grant her heart's desire
   In fulness of *her* will !

V.

THE WIDOW OF NAIN.

FORTH from the city, with the load
    That makes the trampling low,
They walk along the dreary road
    That dust and ashes go.

The other way, towards the gate,
    Their footsteps light and loud,
A living man, in humble state,
    Brings on another crowd.

Nearer and nearer come the twain;
    He hears the wailing cry:
How can the Life let such a train
    Of death and tears go by?

"Weep not" he said, and touched the bier;
    They stand, the dead who bear;
The mother knows nor hope nor fear,
    He waits not for her prayer.

"Young man, I say to thee, arise."
    Who hears, he must obey;
Up starts the form; wide flash the eyes
    With wonder and dismay.

The lips would speak, as if they caught
    Some converse sudden broke,
When the great word the dead man sought,
    And Hades' silence woke.

The lips would speak: the eyes' wild stare
    Gives place to ordered sight;
The murmur dies upon the air—
    The soul is dumb with light.

He brings no news ; he has forgot,
　　Or saw with vision weak :
Thou seëst all our unseen lot,
　　And yet thou dost not speak.

Keep'st thou the news, as parent might
　　A too good gift, away,
Lest we should neither sleep at night,
　　Nor do our work by day?

His mother has not left a trace
　　Of triumph over grief ;
Her tears alone have found a place
　　Upon the holy leaf.

If gratitude our speech benumb,
　　And joy our laughter quell,
May not Eternity be dumb
　　For things too good to tell?

While her glad arms the lost one hold,
    Question she asketh none;
She trusts for all he leaves untold;
    Enough, to clasp her son.

The ebbing tide is caught and won—
    Borne flowing to the gate;
Death turns him backward to the sun,
    And Life is yet our fate.

VI.

THE WOMAN WHOM SATAN HAD BOUND.

For eighteen years, she, patient soul
   Her eyes hath graveward sent;
All vain for her the starry pole,
   She is so bowed and bent.

What mighty words! Who can be near?
   What tenderness of hands!
Oh! is it strength, or fancy mere?
   New hope, or breaking bands?

The pent life rushes swift along
   Channels it used to know;
And up, amidst the wondering throng,
   She rises firm and slow—

To bend again in grateful awe—
    Will, power no more at strife—
In homage to the living Law
    Who gives her back her life.

Uplifter of the drooping head!
    Unbinder of the bound!
Thou seëst our sore-burdened
    Bend hopeless to the ground.

What if they see thee not, nor cry—
    Thou watchest for the hour
To raise the forward-beaming eye,
    To wake the slumbering power.

I see thee wipe the stains of time
    From off the withered face;
Lift up thy bowed old men, in prime
    Of youthful manhood's grace.

Like summer days from winter's tomb.
   Arise thy women fair;
Old age, a shadow, not a doom,
   Lo! is not anywhere.

All ills of life shall melt away
   As melts a cureless woe,
When, by the dawning of the day
   Surprised, the dream must go.

I think thou, Lord, wilt heal me too,
   Whate'er the needful cure;
The great best only thou wilt do,
   And hoping I endure.

VII.

THE WOMAN WHO CAME BEHIND HIM IN THE CROWD.

NEAR him she stole, rank after rank;
   She feared approach too loud;
She touched his garment's hem, and shrank
   Back in the sheltering crowd.

A shame-faced gladness thrills her frame:
   Her twelve years' fainting prayer
Is heard at last; she is the same
   As other women there.

She hears his voice. He looks about.
   Ah! is it kind or good
To drag her secret sorrow out
   Before that multitude?

The eyes of men she dares not meet—
    On her they straight must fall :
Forward she sped, and at his feet
    Fell down, and told him all.

His presence makes a holy place ;
    No alien eyes are there ;
Her shrinking shame finds godlike grace
    The covert of its care.

"Daughter," he said, "be of good cheer ;
    Thy faith hath made thee whole."
With plenteous love, not healing mere,
    He would content her soul.

VIII.

THE WIDOW WITH THE TWO MITES.

Here *much* and *little* shift and change,
    With scale of need and time;
There *more* and *less* have meanings strange,
    Nor with our reason rhyme.

Sickness may be more hale than health,
    And service kingdom high;
Yea, poverty be bounty's wealth,
    To give like God thereby.

Bring forth your riches; let them go,
    Nor mourn the lost control;
For if ye hoard them, surely so
    Their rust will reach your soul.

Cast in your coins, for God delights
   When from wide hands they fall ;
But here is one who brings two mites,
   And yet gives more than all.

She heard not, she, the mighty praise
   Went home to care and need :
Perhaps the knowledge still delays,
   And yet she has the meed.

IX.

THE WOMEN WHO MINISTERED UNTO HIM.

Enough he labours for his hire;
    Yea, nought can pay his pain;
But powers that wear and waste and tire,
    Need strength to toil again.

They give him freely all they can;
    They give him clothes and food;
In this rejoicing, that the man
    Is not ashamed they should.

High love takes form in lowly thing;
    He knows the offering such;
To them 'tis little that they bring,
    To him 'tis very much.

X.

PILATE'S WIFE.

Why came in dreams the low-born man
   Between thee and thy rest;
For vain thy whispered message ran,
   Though justice was thy quest?

Did some young ignorant angel dare—
   Not knowing what must be,
Or blind with agony of care—
   To fly for help to thee?

It may be. Rather I believe,
   Thou, nobler than thy spouse,
The rumoured grandeur didst receive,
   And sit with pondering brows,

Until thy maidens' gathered tale
   With possible marvel teems :
Thou sleepest, and the prisoner pale
   Returneth in thy dreams.

Well mightst thou suffer things not few
   For his sake all the night !
In pale eclipse he suffers, who
   Is of the world the light.

Precious it were to know thy dream
   Of such a one as he !
Perhaps of him we, waking, deem
   As poor a verity.

XL.

THE WOMAN OF SAMARIA.

In the hot noon, for water cool,
   She strayed in listless mood:
When back she ran, her pitcher full
   Forgot behind her stood.

Like one who followed straying sheep,
   A weary man she saw,
Who sat upon the well so deep,
   And nothing had to draw.

"Give me to drink," he said. Her hand
   Was ready with reply;
From out the old well of the land
   She drew him plenteously.

He spake as never man before ;
  She stands with open ears ;
He spake of holy days in store,
  Laid bare the vanished years.

She cannot still her throbbing heart ;
  She hurries to the town,
And cries aloud in street and mart,
  "The Lord is here: come down."

Her life before was strange and sad,
  Its tale a dreary sound :
Ah ! let it go—or good or bad,
  She has the Master found.

XII.

MARY MAGDALENE.

WITH eyes aglow, and aimless zeal,
    She hither, thither, goes;
Her speech, her motions, all reveal
    A mind without repose.

She climbs the hills, she haunts the sea,
    By madness tortured, driven;
One hour's forgetfulness would be
    A gift from very heaven.

The night brings sleep, sleep new distress;
    The anguish of the day
Returns as free, in darker dress,
    In more secure dismay.

MARY MAGDALENE:

The demons blast her to and fro;
    She has no quiet place;
Enough a woman still to know
    A haunting dim disgrace.

Hers in no other eyes confide
    For even a moment brief;
With restless glance they turn aside,
    Lest they betray her grief.

A human touch! a pang of death!
    And in a low delight
Thou liest, waiting for new breath,
    For morning out of night.

Thou risest up: the earth is fair,
    The wind is cool and free;
Is it a dream of hell's despair
    Dissolves in ecstasy?

Did this man touch thee? Eyes divine
   Make sunrise in thy soul;
Thou seëst love and order shine :—
   His health hath made thee whole.

What matter that the coming time
   Will stain thy virgin name!
Will call thine agony thy crime,
   And count thy madness blame!

Let the reproach of men abide!
   He shall be well content
To see not seldom by his side
   Thy head serenely bent.

Thou sharing in the awful doom,
   Shalt help thy Lord to die;
And, mourning o'er his empty tomb,
   First share his victory.

XIII.

THE WOMAN IN THE TEMPLE.

A STILL dark joy! A sudden face!
    Cold daylight, footsteps, cries!
The temple's naked, shining space,
    Aglare with judging eyes!

All in abandoned guilty hair,
    With terror-pallid lips,
To vulgar scorn her honour bare,
    To vulgar taunts and quips,

Her eyes she fixes on the ground,
    Her shrinking soul to hide:
Lest, at uncurtained windows found,
    Its shame be clear descried.

All-idle hang her listless hands
    And tingle with the shame ;
She sees not who beside her stands,
    She is so bowed with blame.

He stoops, he writes upon the ground,
    Regards nor priests nor wife ;
An awful silence spreads around,
    And wakes an inward strife.

Is it a voice that speaks for thee?
    Almost she hears aghast :
" Let him who from this sin is free,
    At her the first stone cast."

Astonished, waking, growing sad,
    Her eyes bewildered rose ;
She saw the one true friend she had,
    Who loves her though he knows.

THE WOMAN IN THE TEMPLE.

Upon her deathlike, ashy face,
   The blushes rise and spread :
No greater wonder sure had place
   When Lazarus left the dead !

He stoops. In every charnel breast
   Dead conscience rises slow :
They, dumb before that awful guest,
   Turn, one by one, and go.

Alone with him ! Yet no new dread
   Invades the silence round ;
False pride, false shame, all false is dead ;
   She has the Master found.

Who else had spoken on her side,
   Those cruel men withstood ?
From him even shame she would not hide ;
   For him she *will* be good.

He rises—sees the temple bare ;
   They two are left alone.
He turns and asks her, "Woman, where
   Are thine accusers gone?

"Hath none condemned thee?" "Master, no,"
   She answers, trembling sore.
"Neither do I condemn thee. Go,
   And sin not any more."

She turned and went.—To hope and grieve?
   Be what she had not been?
We are not told; but I believe
   His kindness made her clean.

Our sins to thee us captive hale—
   Offences, hatreds dire ;
Weak loves that selfish grow, and fail
   And fall into the mire.

Our conscience-cry with pardon meet;
  Our passion cleanse with pain;
Lord, thou didst make these miry feet—
  Oh! wash them clean again.

XIV.

MARTHA.

WITH joyful pride her heart is high:
   Her humble chambers hold
The man prophetic destiny
   Long centuries hath foretold.

Poor, is he? Yes, and lowly born:
   Her woman-soul is proud
To know and hail the coming morn
   Before the eyeless crowd.

At her poor table will he eat?
   He shall be served there
With honour and devotion meet
   For any king that were.

'Tis all she can; she does her part,
    Profuse in sacrifice;
Nor knows that in her unknown heart
    A better offering lies.

But many crosses she must bear;
    Her plans are turned and bent;
Do all she can, things will not wear
    The form of her intent.

With idle hands, and drooping lid,
    See Mary sit at rest!
Shameful it was her sister did
    No service for their guest.

But Martha one day Mary's lot
    Must share with hands and eyes;
Must—all her household cares forgot—
    Sit down as idly wise.

Ere long they both in Jesus' ear
    Shall make the self-same moan :
"Lord, if thou only hadst been here,
    My brother had not gone."

Then once will Martha set her word,
    Yet once, to bar his ways,
Crying, "By this he stinketh, Lord :
    He hath been dead four days."

When Lazarus drags his trammelled clay
    Forth with half-opened eyes,
Her buried best will hear, obey
    And with the dead man rise.

XV.

MARY.

I.

She sitteth at the Master's feet
    In motionless employ;
Her ears, her heart, her soul complete
    Drinks in the tide of joy.

Ah! who but her the glory knows
    Of life, pure, high, intense,
Whose holy calm breeds awful shows
    Beyond the realm of sense!

In her still ear, his thoughts of grace
    Incarnate are in voice;
Her thoughts, the people of the place,
    Receive them, and rejoice.

Her eyes, with heavenly reason bright,
    Are on the ground cast low;
It is his words of truth and light
    That sets them shining so.

But see! a face is at the door
    Whose eyes are not at rest;
A voice breaks in on wisest lore
    With petulant request.

"Lord," Martha says, "dost thou not care
    She lets me serve alone?
Tell her to come and take her share."
    Still Mary's eyes shine on.

Calmly she lifts a questioning glance
    To him who calmly heard;
The merest sign, she'll rise at once,
    Nor wait the uttered word.

The other, standing by the door,
  Waits too what he will say.
His "Martha, Martha" with it bore
  A sense of coming *nay*.

Gently her troubled heart he chid;
  Rebuked its needless care;
Methinks her face she turned and hid,
  With shame that bordered prayer.

What needful thing is Mary's choice,
  Nor shall be taken away?
There is but one—'tis Jesus' voice;
  And listening she shall stay.

Oh, joy to every doubting heart,
  Doing the thing it would,
When he, the holy, takes its part,
  And calls its choice the good!

2.

Not now the living words are poured
    Into her single heart;
For many guests are at the board,
    And many tongues take part.

With sacred foot, refrained and slow,
    With daring, trembling tread,
She comes, with worship bending low
    Behind the godlike head.

The costly chrism, in snowy stone,
    A gracious odour sends.
Her little hoard, so slowly grown,
    In one full act she spends.

She breaks the box, the honoured thing !
   And down its riches pour ;
Her priestly hands anoint her king,
   To reign for evermore.

With murmur and nod, they called it waste :
   Their love they could endure ;
Hers ached a prisoner in her breast,
   And she forgot the poor.

She meant it for his coming state
   He took it for his doom.
The other women were too late,
   For he had left the tomb

XVI.

THE WOMAN THAT WAS A SINNER.

His face, his words, her heart awoke;
    Awoke her slumbering truth;
She judged him well; her bonds she broke,
    And fled to him for ruth.

With tears she washed his weary feet;
    She wiped them with her hair;
Her kisses—call them not unmeet,
    When they were welcome *there*.

What saint—a richer crown to throw,
    Could love's ambition teach?
Her eyes, her lips, her hair, down go,
    In love's despair of speech.

His holy manhood's perfect worth
    Owns her a woman still;
It is impossible henceforth
    For her to stoop to ill.

Her to herself his words restore,
    The radiance to the day;
A horror to herself no more,
    Not yet a cast-away!

And so, in kisses, ointment, tears,
    And outspread lavish hair,
Love, shame, and hope, and griefs, and fears
    Mingle in worship rare.

Mary, thy hair thou didst not spread
    About the holy feet;
Didst only bless the holy head
    With spikenard's ointment sweet.

Or if thou didst, as some would hold—
  Thy heart the lesson caught,
The abandonment so humble-bold,
  From her whom pardon taught.

And if thy hair thou too didst wind
  The holy feet around,
Such plenteous tears thou couldst not find
  As this sad woman found.

Let her in grief the first be read—
  And love, the woful sweet !
Be thou content to bless his head,
  Let this one crown his feet.

Simon, her kisses will not soil ;
  Her tears are pure as rain ;
Eye not her hair's untwisted coil,
  Baptized in pardoning pain.

For God hath pardoned all her *much*;
    Her iron bands hath burst;
Her love could never have been such,
    Had not his love been first.

But oh! rejoice, ye sisters pure,
    Who hardly know her case:
There is no sin but has its cure,
    Its all-consuming grace.

He did not leave her soul in hell,
    'Mong shards the silver dove;
But raised her pure that she might tell
    Her sisters how to love.

She gave him all your best love can.
    Was he despised and sad?—
Yes; and yet never mighty man
    Such perfect homage had.

Jesus, by whose forgiveness sweet,
   Her love grew so intense,
We, sinners all, come round thy feet—
   Lord, make no difference.

A BOOK OF SONNETS.

A BOOK OF SONNETS.

THE BURNT OFFERING.

THRICE-HAPPY he, whose heart, each
    new-born night,
  When the worn day hath vanished o'er
earth's brim,
And he hath laid him down in chamber dim,
Straightway begins to tremble and grow bright,
And loose faint flashes towards the vaulted height
Of the great peace that overshadows him,
Till tongues of fiery hope awake and swim
Thorough his soul, and touch each point with light.
Then the great earth a holy altar is,
Upon whose top a sacrifice he lies,

Burning in love's response up to the skies
Whose fire descended first and kindled his:
When slow the flickering flames at length expire,
Sleep's ashes only hide the glowing fire.

THE UNSEEN FACE.

"I do beseech thee, God, show me thy face."
"Come up to me in Sinai on the morn:
Thou shalt behold as much as may be borne."
And on a rock stood Moses, lone in space.
From Sinai's top, the vaporous, thunderous place,
God passed in cloud, an earthly garment worn
To hide, and thus reveal. In love, not scorn,
He put him in a clift of the rock's base,
Covered him with his hand, his eyes to screen—
Passed—lifted it—his back alone appears.
Ah, Moses! had he turned, and hadst thou seen
The pale face crowned with thorns, baptized with
      tears,
The eyes of the true man, by men belied,
Thou hadst beheld God's face, and straightway died.

CONCERNING JESUS.

I.

IF thou hadst been a sculptor, what a race
Of forms divine had thenceforth filled the land!
Methinks I see thee, glorious workman, stand,
Striking a marble window through blind space;
Thy face's reflex on the coming face,
As dawns the stone to statue 'neath thy hand—
Body obedient to its soul's command,
Which is thy thought informing it with grace!
So had it been. But God, who quickeneth clay,
Nor turneth it to marble—maketh eyes,
Not shadowy hollows, where no sunbeams play,
Would mould his loftiest thought in human guise:
Thou didst appear, walking unknown abroad,
God's living sculpture, all-informed of God.

II.

IF one should say, "Lo, there thy statue! take
Possession, sculptor; now inherit it;
Go forth upon the earth in likeness fit;
As with a trumpet-cry at morning, wake
The sleeping nations; with light's terror, shake
The slumber from their hearts, that, where they sit,
They leap straight up, aghast, as at a pit
Gaping beneath;" I hear him answer make:
"Alas for me! for I nor can nor dare
Inform what I revered as I did trace.
'Twere scorn, inspired truth so to impair,
With feeble spirit mocking the enorm
Strength on its forehead." Thou, God's thought thy form,
Didst live the large significance of thy face.

III.

Men have I seen, and seen with wonderment,
Noble in form, " lift upward and divine,"*
In whom I yet must search, as in a mine,
After that soul of theirs, by which they went
Alive upon the earth.   And I have bent
Regard on many a woman, who gave sign
God willed her beautiful, when he drew the line
That shaped each float and fold of beauty's tent :
Her soul, alas! chambered in pigmy space,
Left the fair visage pitiful inane—
Poor signal only of a coming face
When from the penetrale she filled the fane.
Possessed of thee was every form of thine—
Thy very hair replete with the divine.

* Marlowe's *Tamburlaine the Great*.

IV

IF thou hadst built a temple, how my eye
Had greedily worshipped, from the low-browed crypt
Up to the soaring pinnacles that, tipt
With stars, made signals when the sun drew nigh!
Dark caverns in and under; vivid sky
Its home and aim! Say, from the glory slipt,
And down into the shadows dropt and dipt,
Or reared from darkness up so holy-high?
'Tis man himself, the temple of thy Ghost,
From hidden origin to hidden fate—
Foot in the grave, head in blue spaces great—
From grave and sky filled with a fighting host.
Fight glooms and glory? or does the glory borrow
Strength from the hidden glory of to-morrow?

V.

If thou hadst been a painter, what fresh looks,
What outbursts of pent glories, what new grace
Had shone upon us from the great world's face!
How had we read, as in new-languaged books,
Clear love of God in loneliest shiest nooks!
A lily, if thy hand its form did trace,
Had plainly been God's child, of lower race;—
How strong the hills, how sweet the grassy brooks!
To thee all nature open lay, and bare,
Because thy soul was nature's inner side;
Clear as the world on the dawn's golden tide,
Its vast idea in thy soul did rise;
Thine was the earth, thine all her meanings rare—
The ideal Man, with the eternal eyes!

VI.

But I have seen pictures the work of man,
In which at first appeared but chaos wild :
So high the art transcended, they beguiled
The eye as formless, and without a plan.
Not soon the spirit, brooding o'er, began
To see a purpose rise, like mountain isled,
When God said, Let the Dry appear! and, piled
Above the waves, it rose in twilight wan.
So might thy pictures then have been too strange
For us to pierce beyond their outmost look ;
A vapour and a darkness ; a sealed book ;
An atmosphere too high for wings to range ;
Where gazing must our spirits pale and change,
And tremble as at a void thought cannot brook.

VII.

But earth is now thy living picture, where
Thou shadowest truth, the simple and profound
By the same form in vital union bound :
Where one can see but the first step of thy stair,
Another sees it vanish far in air.
When thy king David viewed the starry round,
From heart and fingers broke the psaltery-sound :
Lord, what is man, that thou shouldst mind his
    prayer !
But when the child beholds the heavens on high,
He babbles childish noises—not less dear
Than what the king sang praying—to the ear
Of him who made the child and king and sky.
Earth is thy picture, painter great, whose eye
Sees with the child, sees with the kingly seer.

VIII.

If thou hadst built some mighty instrument,
And set thee down to utter ordered sound,
Whose faithful billows, from thy hands unbound,
Breaking in light, against our spirits went,
And caught, and bore above this earthly tent,
The far-strayed back to their prime natal ground,
Where all roots fast in harmony are found,
And God sits thinking out a pure concent;
If—ah! how easy that had been for thee!
Our broken music thou must first restore—
A harder task than think thine own out free;
But till thou hast done it, no divinest score,
Though rendered by thine own angelic choir,
Could lift a human soul from foulest mire.

IX.

If thou hadst been a poet! On my heart
The thought flashed sudden, burning through the
    weft
Of life, and with too much I sank bereft.
Up to my eyes the tears, with sudden start,
Thronged blinding: would the veil now rend and
    part?
The husk of vision—would that in twain be cleft,
Its hidden soul in naked beauty left,
And I behold thee, Nature, as thou art?
O poet Jesus! at thy holy feet
I should have lien, sainted with listening;
My pulses answering ever, in rhythmic beat,
The stroke of each triumphant melody's wing,
Creating, as it moved, my being sweet;
My soul thy harp, thy word the quivering string.

X.

Thee had we followed through the twilight land
Where thought grows form, and matter is refined
Back into thought of the eternal mind,
Till, seeing them one, lo, in the morn we stand!
Then start afresh and follow, hand in hand,
With sense divinely growing, till, combined,
We heard the music of the planets wind
In harmony with billows on the strand!
Till, one with earth and all God's utterance,
We hardly knew whether the sun outspake,
Or a glad sunshine from our spirits brake;
Whether we think, or winds and blossoms dance!
Alas, O poet leader! for such good,
Thou wast God's tragedy, writ in tears and blood.

XI.

Hadst thou been one of these, in many eyes,
Too near to be a glory for thy sheen,
Thou hadst been scorned; and to the best hadst
    been
A setter forth of strange divinities;
But to the few construct of harmonies,
A sudden sun, uplighting the serene
High heaven of love; and, through the cloudy
    screen
That 'twixt our souls and truth all wretched lies
Dawning at length, hadst been a love and fear,
Worshipped on high from magian's mountain-crest,
And all night long symbolled by lamp-flames clear;
Thy sign, a star upon thy people's breast,
Where now a strange mysterious token lies,
That once barred out the sun in noontide skies.

XII.

But as thou camest forth to bring the poor,
Whose hearts are nearer faith and verity,
Spiritual childhood, thy philosophy—
So taught'st the A, B, C of heavenly lore;
Because thou sat'st not lonely evermore,
With mighty thoughts informing language high,
But, walking in thy poem continually,
Didst utter deeds, of all true forms the core—
Poet and poem one indivisible fact;
Because thou didst thine own ideal act,
And so for parchment, on the human soul
Didst write thine aspirations, at thy goal
Thou didst arrive with curses for acclaim,
And cry to God up through a cloud of shame.

XIII.

For three and thirty years, a living seed,
A lonely germ, dropt on our waste world's side,
Thy death and rising thou didst calmly bide;
Sore companied by many a clinging weed
Sprung from the fallow soil of evil and need;
Hither and thither tossed, by friends denied;
Pitied of goodness dull, and scorned of pride;
Until at length was done the awful deed,
And thou didst lie outworn in stony bower
Three days asleep—oh, slumber godlike brief
For man of sorrows and acquaint with grief!
Heaven's seed thou diedst, that out of thee might
    tower
Aloft with rooted stem and shadowy leaf,
Of all humanity the crimson flower.

XIV.

When dim the etherial eye, no art, though clear
As golden star in morning's amber springs,
Can pierce the fogs of low imaginings:
Painting and sculpture are but mockery mere.
When dull to deafness is the hearing ear,
Vain too the poet. Nought but earthly things
Have credence. When the soaring skylark sings
How shall the stony statue strain to hear?
Open the deaf ear, wake the sleeping eye,
And lo, musicians, painters, poets—all
Trooping unsent for, come without a call!
As winds that where they list blow evermore;
As waves from silent deserts roll to die
In mighty voices on the peopled shore.

XV.

Our ears thou openedst; mad'st our eyes to see.
All they who work in stone or colour fair,
Or build up temples of the quarried air,
Which we call music, scholars are of thee.
Henceforth in might of such the earth shall be
Truth's temple-theatre, where she shall wear
All forms of revelation, and they bear
Tapers in acolyte humility.
O Master-maker! thy exultant art
Goes forth in making makers. Pictures? No;
But painters, who in love and truth shall show
Glad secrets from thy God's rejoicing heart.
All-unforetold, green grass and corn up start,
When through dead sands thy living waters go.

XVI.

From the beginning good and fair are one,
But men the beauty from the truth will part,
And, though the truth is ever beauty's heart,
After the beauty will, short-breathed, run,
And the indwelling truth deny and shun.
Therefore, in cottage, synagogue and mart,
Thy thoughts came forth in common speech, not art;
With voice and eye in Jewish Babylon
Thou taughtest—not with pen or carved stone,
Nor in thy hand the trembling wires didst take:
Thou of the truth not less than all wouldst make;
For her sake even her forms thou didst disown :
Ere beauty cause the word of truth to fail,
The light behind shall burn the broidered veil.

XVII.

Holy of holies!—Lord, let me come nigh!
For, Lord, thy body is the shining veil
By which I look on God and am not pale.
Forgive me, if in these poor verses lie
Mean thoughts, for see, the thinker is not high.
But were my song as loud as saints' all-hail,
As pure as prophet's cry of warning wail,
As holy as thy mother's ecstasy,
I know a better thing—for love or ruth,
To my weak heart a little child to take.
Nor thoughts nor feelings, art nor wisdom seal
The man who at thy table bread shall break.
Thy praise was not that thou didst know, or feel,
Or show, or love, but that thou didst the truth.

XVIII.

DESPISED! Rejected by the priest-led roar
Of multitudes! The imperial purple flung
Around the form the hissing scourge had wrung!
To the bare truth dear witnessing, before
The false, and trembling true! As on the shore
Of infinite love and truth, I kneel among
The blood-prints, and with dumb adoring tongue,
Cry to the naked man who erewhile wore
The love-wove garment—" Witness to the truth,
Crowned by thy witnessing, thou art the King!
With thee I die, to live in worshipping.
O human God! O brother, eldest born!
Never but thee was there a man in sooth!
Never a true crown but thy crown of thorn!"

A MEMORIAL OF AFRICA.

I.

Upon a rock I sat—a mountain-side,
Far, far forsaken of the old sea's lip;
A rock where ancient waters' rise and dip,
Recoil and plunge, and backward eddying tide
Had worn and worn, while races lived and died,
Involved channels. Where the sea-weed's drip
Followed the ebb, now crumbling lichens sip
Sparse dews of heaven, that down with sunset slide.
I sat and gazed southwards. A dry flow
Of withering wind sucked up my drooping strength,
Slow gliding from the desert's burning length.
Behind me piled, away and upward go
Great sweeps of savage mountains—up, away,
Where snow gleams ever—panthers roam, they say.

II.

This infant world has taken long to make!
Nor hast Thou done the making of it yet,
But wilt be working on when death has set
A new mound in some churchyard for my sake.
On flow the centuries without a break;
Uprise the mountains, ages without let;
The lichens suck the rock's breast—food they get:
Years more than past, the young earth yet will take.
But in the dumbness of the rolling time,
No veil of silence shall encompass me—
Thou wilt not once forget and let me be;
Rather wouldst thou some old chaotic prime
Invade, and, with a tenderness sublime,
Unfold a world, that I, thy child, might see.

A. M. D.

METHINKS I see thee, lying straight and low,
Silent and darkling, in thy earthy bed,
The mighty strength in which I trusted, fled,
The long arms lying careless of kiss or blow;
On thy tall form I see the night robe flow
Down from the pale, composed face—thy head
Crowned with its own dark curls: though thou wast dead,
They dressed thee as for sleep, and left thee so.
My heart, with cares and questionings oppressed,
Seldom since thou didst leave me, turns to thee;
But wait, my brother, till I too am dead,
And thou shalt find that heart more true, more free,
More ready in thy love to take its rest,
Than when we lay together in one bed.

TO GARIBALDI.

(WITH A BOOK—WHEN HE VISITED ENGLAND.)

When, at Philippi, he who would have freed
Great Rome from tyrants, for the season brief
That lay 'twixt him and battle, sought relief
From painful thoughts, he in a book did read,
That so the death of Portia might not breed
Too many thoughts, and cloud his mind with grief:
Brother of Brutus, of high hearts the chief,
When thou in heaven receiv'st the heavenly meed,
And I shall find my hoping not in vain,
Tell me my book has wiled away one pang
That out of some lone sacred memory sprang,
Or wrought an hour's forgetfulness of pain,
And I shall rise, my heart brimful of gain,
And thank my God amid the golden clang.

TO S. F. S.

They say that lonely sorrows do not chance.
It may be true; one thing I think I know:
New sorrow joins a gliding funeral slow
With less jar than it shocks a merry dance.
But if griefs troop, why, joy doth joy enhance
As often, and the balance levels so.
If quick to see flowers by the wayside blow,
As quick to feel the lurking thorns that lance
The foot that walketh naked in the way,—
Blest by the lily, white from toils and fears,
Oftener than wounded by the thistle-spears,
We should walk upright, bold, and earnest-gay
And when the last night closed on the last day,
Should sleep like one that far-off music hears.

ORGAN SONGS.

TO A. J. SCOTT

WITH THE FOLLOWING POEM.

I WALKED all night: the darkness did
    not yield.
Around me fell a mist, a weary rain,
Enduring long. At length the dawn revealed

A temple's front, high-lifted from the plain.
Closed were the lofty doors that led within;
But by a wicket one might entrance gain.

'Twas awe and silence. When I entered in,
The night, the weariness, the rain were lost
In hopeful spaces. First I heard a thin

Sweet sound of voices low, together tossed,
As if they sought some harmony to find
Which they knew once, but none of all that host

Could wile the far-fled music back to mind.
Loud voices, distance-low, wandered along
The pillared paths, and up the arches twined

With sister-arches, rising, throng on throng,
Up to the roof's dim height.   At broken times
The voices gathered to a burst of song,

But parted sudden, and were but single rhymes
By single bells through Sabbath morning sent,
That have no thought of harmony or chimes.

Hopeful confusion!   Who could be content
Looking and listening only by the door?
I entered further.   Solemnly it went—

TO A. J. SCOTT.

Thy voice, Truth's herald, walking the untuned
    roar,
Calm and distinct, powerful and sweet and fine:
I loved and listened, listened and loved more.

If the weak harp may, tremulous, combine
Faint ghostlike sounds with organ's loudest tone,
Let my poor song be taken in to thine.

Thy heart, with organ-tempests of its own,
Will hear æolian sighs from thin chords blown.

LIGHT.

First-born of the creating Voice!
Minister of God's Spirit, who wast sent
Waiting upon him first, what time he went
Moving about 'mid the tumultuous noise
Of each unpiloted element
Upon the face of the void formless deep!
Thou who didst come unbodied and alone,
Ere yet the sun was set his rule to keep,
Or ever the moon shone,
Or e'er the wandering star-flocks forth were driven!
Thou garment of the Invisible, whose skirt
Sweeps, glory-giving, over earth and heaven!
Thou comforter, be with me as thou wert

LIGHT.

When first I longed for words, to be
A radiant garment for my thought, like thee.

We lay us down in sorrow,
Wrapt in the old mantle of our mother Night;
In vexing dreams we strive until the morrow;
Grief lifts our eyelids up—and lo, the light!
The sunlight on the wall! And visions rise
Of shining leaves that make sweet melodies;
Of wind-borne waves with thee upon their crests
Of rippled sands on which thou rainest down;
Of quiet lakes that smooth for thee their breasts;
Of clouds that show thy glory as their own;
O joy! O joy! the visions are gone by!
Light, gladness, motion, are reality!

Thou art the god of earth. The skylark springs
Far up to catch thy glory on his wings;

And thou dost bless him first that highest soars.
The bee comes forth to see thee; and the flowers
Worship thee all day long, and through the skies
Follow thy journey with their earnest eyes.
River of life, thou pourest on the woods,
And on thy waves float out the wakening buds.
The trees lean towards thee, and, in loving pain,
Keep turning still to see thee yet again.
And nothing in thine eyes is mean or low:
Where'er thou art, on every side,
All things are glorified;
And where thou canst not come, there thou dost throw
Beautiful shadows, made out of the dark,
That else were shapeless; now it bears thy mark.

And men have worshipped thee.
The Persian, on his mountain-top,
Waits kneeling till thy sun go up,

God-like in his serenity.
All-giving, and none-gifted, he draws near;
And the wide earth waits till his face appear—
Longs patient. And the herald glory leaps
Along the ridges of the outlying clouds,
Climbing the heights of all their towering steeps;
Till a quiet multitudinous laughter crowds
The universal face, and, silently,
Up cometh he, the never-closing eye.
Symbol of Deity! men could not be
Farthest from truth when they were kneeling unto
    thee

  Thou plaything of the child,
When from the water's surface thou dost spring,
Thyself upon his chamber ceiling fling,
And there, in mazy dance and motion wild,
Disport thyself—etherial, undefiled,
Capricious, like the thinkings of the child!

I am a child again, to think of thee
In thy consummate glee.
Or, through the gray dust darting in long streams,
How I would play with thee, athirst to climb
On sloping ladders of thy moted beams!
How marvel at the dusky glimmering red,
With which my closed fingers thou hadst made
Like rainy clouds that curtain the sun's bed!
And how I loved thee always in the moon!
But most about the harvest-time,
When corn and moonlight made a mellow tune,
And thou wert grave and tender as a cooing dove!
And then the stars that flashed cold, deathless love!
And the ghost-stars that shimmered in the tide!
And more mysterious earthly stars,
That shone from windows of the hill and glen—
Thee prisoned in with lattice-bars,
Mingling with household love and rest of weary
    men!

And still I am a child, thank God!—to spy
Thee starry stream from bit of broken glass,
Upon the brown earth undescried,
Is a found thing to me, a gladness high,
A spark that lights joy's altar-fire within,
A thought of hope to prophecy akin,
And from my spirit fruitless will not pass.

Thou art the joy of age:
Thy sun is dear when long the shadow falls.
Forth to its friendliness the old man crawls,
And, like the bird hung out in his poor cage
To gather song from radiance, in his chair
Sits by the door; and sitteth there
His soul within him, like a child that lies
Half dreaming, with half-open eyes,
At close of a long afternoon in summer—
High ruins round him, ancient ruins, where
The raven is almost the only comer;

Half dreams, half broods, in wonderment
At thy celestial descent,
Through rifted loops alighting on the gold
That waves its bloom in many an airy rent :
So dreams the old man's soul, that is not old,
But sleepy 'mid the ruins that infold.

What soul-like changes, evanescent moods,
Upon the face of the still passive earth,
Its hills, and fields, and woods,
Thou with thy seasons and thy hours art ever call-
    ing forth !
Even like a lord of music bent
Over his instrument,
Who gives to tears and smiles an equal birth !
When clear as holiness the morning ray
Casts the rock's dewy darkness at its feet,
Mottling with shadows all the mountain gray ;
When, at the hour of sovereign noon,

Infinite silent cataracts sheet
Shadowless through the air of thunder-breeding
    June;
And when a yellower glory slanting passes
'Twixt longer shadows o'er the meadow grasses;
When now the moon lifts up her shining shield,
High on the peak of a cloud-hill revealed;
Now crescent, low, wandering sun-dazed away,
Unconscious of her own star-mingled ray,
Her still face seeming more to think than see,
Makes the pale world lie dreaming dreams of thee!
No mood of mind, no melody of soul,
But lies within thy silent soft control.

   Of operative single power,
And simple unity the one emblem,
Yet all the colours that our passionate eyes devour,
In rainbow, moonbow, or in opal gem,
Are the melodious descant of divided thee.

Lo thee in yellow sands! lo thee
In the blue air and sea!
In the green corn, with scarlet poppies lit,
Thy half-souls parted, patient thou dost sit.
Lo thee in speechless glories of the west!
Lo thee in dew-drop's tiny breast!
Thee on the vast white cloud that floats away,
Bearing upon its skirt a brown moon-ray!
Regent of colour, thou dost fling
Thy overflowing skill on every thing!
The thousand hues and shades upon the flowers,
Are all the pastime of thy leisure hours;
And all the jewelled ores in mines that hidden be,
Are dead till touched by thee.

   Everywhere,
Thou art lancing through the air;
Every atom from another
Takes thee, gives thee to his brother;

LIGHT.

Continually,
Thou art wetting the wet sea,
Bathing its sluggish woods below,
Making the salt flowers bud and blow;
Silently,
Workest thou, and ardently,
Waking from the night of nought
Into being and to thought;
Influences
Every beam of thine dispenses,
Potent, subtle, reaching far,
Shooting different from each star.
Not an iron rod can lie
In circle of thy beamy eye,
But thy look doth change it so
That it cannot choose but show
Thou, the worker, hast been there;
Yea, sometimes, on substance rare,
Thou dost leave thy ghostly mark

Even in what men call the dark.
Doer, shower, mighty teacher!
Truth-in-beauty's silent preacher!
Universal something sent
To shadow forth the Excellent!

When the firstborn affections—
Those winged seekers of the world within,
That search about in all directions,
Some bright thing for themselves to win—
Through pathless forests, gathering fogs,
Through stony plains, treacherous bogs,
Long, long, have followed faces fair,
Fair soul-less faces which have vanished into air;
And darkness is around them and above,
Desolate, with nought to love;
And through the gloom on every side,
Strange dismal forms are dim descried;
And the air is as the breath

From the lips of void-eyed Death;
And the knees are bowed in prayer
To the Stronger than despair;
Then the ever-lifted cry,
Give us light, or we shall die,
Cometh to the Father's ears,
And he hearkens, and he hears;
And slow, as if some sun would glimmer forth
From sunless winter of the north,
They, hardly trusting happy eyes,
Discern a dawning in the skies:
'Tis Truth awaking in the soul;
Thy Righteousness to make them whole.
—What shall men, this Truth adoring,
Gladness giving, youth-restoring,
Call it but eternal Light?—
'Tis the morning, 'twas the night.
Even a misty hope that lies on
Our dim future's far horizon,

We call a fresh aurora, sent
Up the spirit's firmament.
Telling, through the vapours dun,
Of the coming, coming sun.

   All things most excellent
Are likened unto thee, excellent thing !
Yea, he who from the Father forth was sent,
Came like a lamp, to bring,
Across the winds and wastes of night,
The everlasting light ;
The Word of God, the telling of his thought ;
The Light of God, the making-visible ;
The far-transcending glory brought
In human form with man to dwell ;
The dazzling gone ; the power not less
To show, irradiate, and bless ;
The gathering of the primal rays divine,
Informing chaos, to a pure sunshine !

LIGHT.

Dull horrid pools no motion making!
No bubble on the surface breaking!
The heavy dead air gives no sound,
Asleep and moveless on the marshy ground.

Rushing winds and snow-like drift,
Forceful, formless, fierce, and swift!
Hair-like vapours madly riven!
Waters smitten into dust!
Lightning through the turmoil driven,
Aimless, useless, yet it must!

Gentle winds through forests calling!
Bright birds through the thick leaves glancing!
Solemn waves on sea-shores falling!
White sails on blue waters dancing!
Mountain streams glad music giving!
Children in the clear pool laving!
Yellow corn and green grass waving!

Long-haired, bright-eyed maidens living !
Light, O Radiant ! it is thou !
And we know our Father now.

Forming ever without form ;
Showing, but thyself unseen ;
Pouring stillness on the storm ;
Making life where death had been !
Light, if He did draw thee in,
Death and Chaos soon were out,
Weltering o'er the slimy sea,
Riding on the whirlwind's rout,
In unmaking energy !
Thou art round us, God within,
Fighting darkness, slaying sin.

Father of Lights, high-lost, unspeakable
On whom no changing shadow ever fell !
Thy light we know not, are content to see ;

And shall we doubt because we know not thee?
Or, when thy wisdom cannot be expressed,
Fear lest dark vapours brood within thy breast?
It shall not be;
Our hearts awake and speak aloud for thee.
The very shadows on our souls that lie,
Good witness to the light supernal bear;
The something 'twixt us and the sky
Could cast no shadow if light were not there.
If children tremble in the night,
It is because their God is light.
The shining of the common day
Is mystery still, howe'er it ebb and flow
Behind the seeing orb, the secret lies:
Thy living light's eternal play,
Its motions, whence or whither, who shall know?—
Behind the life itself, its fountains rise.

    Enlighten me, O Light!—why ar' thou such?

Why art thou awful to our eyes, and sweet *
Cherished as love, and slaying with a touch?
Why in thee do the known and unknown meet?
Why swift and tender, strong and delicate?
Simple as truth, yet manifold in might?
Why does one love thee, and another hate?
Why cleave my words to the portals of my speech,
When I a goodly matter would indite?
Why fly my thoughts themselves beyond my reach?
—In vain to follow thee, I thee beseech,
For God is light.

TO A. J. SCOTT.

Thus, once, long since, the daring of my youth
Drew nigh thy greatness with a little thing.
Thou didst receive me; and thy sky of truth

Has domed me since, a heaven of sheltering,
Made homely by the tenderness and grace
Which round thy absolute friendship ever fling

A radiant atmosphere. Turn not thy face
From that small part of earnest thanks, I pray,
Which, spoken, leaves much more in speechless
    case.

I see thee far before me on thy way
Up the great peaks, and striding stronger still
Thy intellect unrivalled in its sway,

Upheld and ordered by a regnant will ;
Thy wisdom, seer and priest of holy fate,
Searching all truths, its prophecy to fill ;

But, O my friend, throned in thy heart so great.
High Love is queen, and hath no equal mate.

   May, 1857.

I WOULD I WERE A CHILD.

I would I were a child,
That I might look, and laugh, and say, My Father!
And follow thee with running feet, or rather
    Be led through dark and wild.

How I would hold thy hand,
My glad eyes often to thy glory lifting!
Should darkness 'twixt thy face and mine come drifting,
    How hearken thy command!

If an ill thing came near,
I would but creep within thy mantle's folding,
Shut my eyes close, thy hand yet faster holding,
    And thus forget my fear.

O soul, O soul, rejoice!
Thou art God's child indeed, for all thy sinning;
A poor weak child, yet his, and worth the winning
   With saviour eyes and voice.

Who spoke the words? Didst Thou?
They are too good, even for such a giver:
Such water drinking once, I must feel ever
   As I had drunk but now.

Yet sure he taught us so,
Teaching our lips to say with his, Our Father!
Telling the tale of wanderer who did gather
   His goods to him, and go!

Ah! thou dost lead me, God;
But it is dark; no stars! the way is dreary;
Almost I sleep, I am so very weary
   Upon this rough hill-road.

Almost! Nay, I *do* sleep;
There is no darkness save in this my dreaming;
Thy fatherhood above, around, is beaming;
   Thy hand my hand doth keep.

Cast on my face one gleam;
I have no knowledge but that I am sleeping;
Lost in its lies, my life goes out in weeping;
   Wake me from this my dream.

How long shall heavy night
Deny the day? How long shall this dull sorrow
Say in my heart that never any morrow
   Will bring the vanished light?

Lord, art thou in the room?
Come near my bed; oh! draw aside the curtain;
A child's heart would say *Father*, were it certain
   The word would not presume.

But if this dreary sleep
May not be broken, help thy helpless sleeper
To rest in thee; so shall his sleep grow deeper—
   For evil dreams too deep.

Father! I dare at length;
My childhood sure will shield me from all blaming:
Sinful, yet hoping, I to thee come, claiming
   Thy tenderness, my strength.

A PRAYER FOR THE PAST.

All sights and sounds of day and year,
All groups and forms, each leaf and gem,
Are thine, O God, nor will I fear
To talk to thee of them.

Too great thy heart is to despise;
Thy day girds centuries about;
From things we little call, thine eyes
See great things looking out.

Therefore the prayerful song I sing
May come to thee in ordered words;
Its low-born echo shall not cling
In terror to the chords.

*I think that nothing made is lost;
That not a moon has ever shone,
That not a cloud my eyes hath crossed
But to my soul is gone.*

*That all the lost years garnered lie
In this thy casket, my dim soul;
And thou wilt, once, the key apply,
And show the shining whole.*

*But were they dead in me, they live
In thee, whose Parable is—Time,
And Worlds, and Forms, and Sounds that give
Thee back the offered rhyme.*

*And after what men call my death,
When I have crossed the unknown sea,
Some heavenly morn, on hopeful breath,
Shall rise this prayer to thee.*

O let me be a child once more,
To dream the glories of the gloom,
The climbing suns and starry store
That ceiled my little room.

O call again the moons that crossed
Blue gulfs, behind gray vapours crept ;
Show me the solemn skies I lost
Because in thee I slept.

Once more let gathering glory swell,
And lift the world's dim eastern eye ;
Once more in twilight's bosoming spell
The western close and die.

But show me first—oh, blessed sight !
The lowly house where I was young ;
There winter sent wild winds at night,
And up the snow-heaps flung ;

Or soundless built a chaos, fair
With lovely wastes and lawless forms,
With ghostly trees and sparkling air—
New sport for white-robed storms.

But, lo! there dawned a dewy morn;
A man was turning up the mould;
And in our hearts the spring was born,
Crept hither through the cold.

On with the glad year let me go,
With troops of daisies round my feet;
Flying my kite, or, in the glow
Of arching summer heat,

Outstretched in fear upon the bank,
Lest, gazing up on awful space,
I should fall down into the blank,
From off the round world's face.

And let my brothers come with me
To play our old games yet again,
Children on earth, more full of glee
That we in heaven are men.

If over us the shade of death
Pass like a cloud across the sun,
We'll tell a secret, in low breath:
" Soon will the *dream* be done.

" 'Tis in the dream our brother's gone
Up stairs: he heard our father call;
For one by one we go alone,
Till he has gathered all."

Father, in joy our knees we bow;
This earth is not a place of tombs:
We are but in the nursery now;
They in the upper rooms.

For are we not at home in thee,
And all this world a visioned show;
That, knowing what Abroad is, we
What Home is, too, may know?

And at thy feet I sit, O Lord,
As once I sat, in moonlight pale,
Hearing my father's measured word
Read out a lofty tale.

Then in the vision let me go
On, onward through the gliding years;
Gathering great noontide's joyous glow,
Eve's love-contented tears;

One afternoon sit pondering
In that old chair, in that old room,
Where passing pigeon's sudden wing
Flashed lightning through the gloom;

There try once more, with effort vain,
To mould in one perplexed things;
There find the solace yet again
Faith in the Father brings;

Or mount and ride in sun and wind,
Through desert moors, hills bleak and high:
There wandering vapours fall, and find
In me another sky.

For so thy Visible grew mine,
Though half its power I could not know;
And in me wrought a work divine,
Which thou hadst ordered so;

Filling my heart with shape and word
From thy full utterance unto men;
Forms that with ancient truth accord,
And find it words again.

*But if thou give me thus the past—
Spring to thy summer leading in,
I now bethink me at the last—
O Lord, leave out the sin.*

*On what I loved my thoughts I bent;
Green leaves unfolding to their fruits,
Expanding flowers, aspiring scent—
Forgot the writhing roots.*

*For Spring, in latest years of youth,
Became the form of every form;
Now bursting joyous into truth,
Now sighing in the storm.*

*Then far from my old northern land,
I lived where gentle winters pass;
Saw green seas lave a wealthy strand,
From hills of unsown grass.*

Saw gorgeous sunsets claim the scope
Of gazing heaven, to spread their show;
Hang scarlet clouds i' th' topmost cope,
With fringes flaming low.

Saw one beside me in whose eyes
Once more old Nature found a home;
There treasured up her changeful skies,
Gray rocks and bursting foam.

But life lies dark before me, God:
Shall I throughout desire to see
And walk once more the hilly road
By which I went to thee?

O'er a new joy this day we bend,
Of lovely power the soul to lift—
A wondering wonder thou dost lend
With loan outpassing gift:

*A little child beholds the sun;
Once more incarnates thy old law—
One born of two, two born in one,
All into one to draw.*

*But is there no day creeping on
Which I should tremble to renew?
I thank thee, Lord, for what is gone—
Thine is the future too.*

*And are we not at home in thee,
And all this world a visioned show;
That knowing what Abroad is, we
What Home is too may know?*

LONGING.

My heart is full of inarticulate pain,
   And beats laborious. Cold ungenial looks
Invade my sanctuary. Men of gain,
   Wise in success, well-read in feeble books,
No nigher come, I pray : your air is drear ;
'Tis winter and low skies when ye appear.

Beloved, who love beauty and fair truth !
   Come nearer me ; too near ye cannot come ;
Make me an atmosphere with your sweet youth ;
   Give me your souls to breathe in, a large room ;
Speak not a word, for see, my spirit lies
Helpless and dumb ; shine on me with your eyes.

O all wide places, far from feverous towns!
　　Great shining seas! pine forests! mountains wild!
Rock-bosomed shores! rough heaths! and sheep-
　　　　cropt downs!
　　Vast pallid clouds! blue spaces undefiled!
Room! give me room! give loneliness and air!
Free things and plenteous in your regions fair.

White dove of David, flying overhead,
　　Golden with sunlight on thy snowy wings,
Outspeeding thee my longing thoughts are fled
　　To find a home afar from men and things;
Where in his temple, earth o'erarched with sky,
God's heart to mine may speak, my heart reply.

O God of mountains, stars, and boundless spaces!
　　O God of freedom and of joyous hearts!
When thy face looketh forth from all men's faces,
　　There will be room enough in crowded marts;

Brood thou around me, and the noise is o'er;
Thy universe my closet with shut door.

Heart, heart, awake! The love that loveth all
    Maketh a deeper calm than Horeb's cave.
God in thee, can his children's folly gall?
    Love may be hurt, but shall not love be brave?—
Thy holy silence sinks in dews of balm;
Thou art my solitude, my mountain-calm.

I KNOW WHAT BEAUTY IS.

I KNOW what beauty is, for Thou
   Hast set the world within my heart ;
   Of me thou madest it a part ;
I never loved it more than now.

I know the Sabbath afternoons ;
   The light asleep upon the graves ;
   Against the sky the poplar waves ;
The river murmurs organ tunes.

I know the spring with bud and bell ;
   The hush in summer woods at night ;
   Autumn, when leaves let in more light ;
Fantastic winter's lovely spell.

I know the rapture music gives,
   The power that dwells in ordered tones;
   Dream-muffled voice, it loves and moans,
And half-alive, comes in and lives.

The charm of verse, where, love-allied,
   Music and thought, in concord high,
   Show many a glory sailing by,
Borne on the Godhead's living tide.

And Beauty's regnant All I know;
   The imperial head, the starry eye;
   The fettered fount of harmony,
That makes the woman radiant go.

But I leave all, thou man of woe!
   Put off my shoes, and come to thee,
   Most beautiful of all I see,
Most wonderful of all I know.

As child forsakes his favourite toy,
   His sisters' sport, his wild bird's nest
   And, climbing to his mother's breast,
Enjoys yet more his former joy—

I lose to find. On white-robed bride
   Fair jewels fairest light afford;
   So, gathered round thy glory, Lord,
All glory else is glorified.

SYMPATHY.

Grief held me silent in my seat;
   I neither moved nor smiled:
Joy held her silent at my feet,
   My shining lily-child.

She raised her face and looked in mine;
   It seemed she was denied;
The door was shut, there was no shine;
   Poor she was left outside.

Once, twice, three times, with infant grace,
   Her lips my name did mould;
Her face was pulling at my face—
   She was but ten months old.

She called the thoughts into the sighs;
    And soon I asked—Does God
Need help from his poor children's eyes,
    To ease him of his load ?

Rarely from love our looks arise—
    Sometimes from needy woe :
If comfort lay in loving eyes,
    He seldom found it so ;

But when we cry in evil case
    From comfort's weary lack,
The weakest hope that seeks his face
    A stronger hope comes back.

Nor waits he, moveless, till we cry,
    But wakes the sleeping prayer;
Not Father only in the sky,
    But servant everywhere.

I looked *not* up ; nor comfort slid
 Downward, my grief to wile :
It was his present face that did
 Smile upward n her smile.

THE THANK-OFFERING.

My Lily snatches not my gift ;
   Hungry she would be fed,
But to her mouth she will not lift
   The piece of broken bread,
Till on my lips, unerring, swift,
   The morsel she has laid.

This is her grace before her food,
   This her libation poured;
Even thus his offering, Aaron good
   Heaved up to thank the Lord,
When for the people all he stood,
   And with a cake adored.*

      * Numbers: xv. 19, 20.

THE THANK-OFFERING.

Our Father, every gift of thine
    I offer at thy knee;
Not else I take the love divine
    With which it comes to me;
Not else the offered grace is mine
    Of being one with thee.

Yea, all my being I would lift,
    An offering of me;
Not yet my very own the gift,
    Till heaved again to thee:
Draw from this dry and narrow clift
    Thy boat upon thy sea.

PRAYER.

We doubt the word that tells us : Ask,
   And ye shall have your prayer ;
We turn our thoughts as to a task,
   With will constrained and rare.

And yet we have ; these scanty prayers
   Yield gold without alloy :
O God ! but he that trusts and dares
   Must have a boundless joy.

REST.

I.

When round the earth the Father's han
 Have gently drawn the dark;
Sent off the sun to fresher lands,
 And curtained in the lark;
'Tis sweet, all tired with glowing day,
 To fade with fading light;
To lie once more, the old weary way,
 Upfolded in the night.

It mothers o'er our slumbers bend,
 And unripe kisses reap,
In soothing dreams with sleep they blend,
 Till even in dreams we sleep.

And if we wake while night is dumb,
  'Tis sweet to turn and say,
It is an hour ere dawning come,
  And I will sleep till day.

II.

There is a dearer, warmer bed,
  Where one all day may lie,
Earth's bosom pillowing the head,
  And let the world go by.
There come no watching mother's eyes;
  The stars instead look down;
Upon it breaks, and silent dies,
  The murmur of the town.

The great world, shouting, forward fares;
  This chamber, hid from none,
Hides safe from all, for no one cares
  For him whose work is done.

Cheer thee, my friend ; bethink thee how
    A certain unknown place,
Or here or there, is waiting now,
    To rest thee from thy race.

III.

Nay, nay, not there the rest from harms,
    The slow composed breath !
Not there the folding of the arms !
    Not there the sleep of death !
It needs no curtained bed to hide
    The world with all its wars ;
No grassy cover to divide
    From sun and moon and stars.

There is a rest that deeper grows
    In midst of pain and strife ;
A mighty, conscious, willed repose,
    The death of deepest life.

To have and hold the precious prize
    No need of jealous bars ;
But windows open to the skies,
    And skill to read the stars.

IV.

Who dwelleth in that secret place,
    Where tumult enters not,
Is never cold with terror base,
    Never with anger hot.
For if an evil host should dare
    His very heart invest,
God is his deeper heart, and there
    He enters in to rest.

When mighty sea-winds madly blow,
    And tear the scattered waves,
Peaceful as summer woods, below
    Lie darkling ocean caves :

REST.

The wind of words may toss my heart,
   But what is that to me!
'Tis but a surface storm—thou art
   My deep, still, resting sea.

O DO NOT LEAVE ME.

O DO not leave me, mother, lest I weep;
Till I forget, be near me in that chair.
The mother's presence leads her down to sleep—
Leaves her contented there.

O do not leave me, lover, brother, friends,
Till I am dead, and resting in my place.
Love-compassed thus, the girl in peace ascends,
And leaves a raptured face.

Leave me not, God, until—nay, until when?
Not till I have with thee one heart, one mind;
Not till the Life is Light in me, and then
Leaving is left behind.

BLESSED ARE THE MEEK, FOR THEY SHALL INHERIT THE EARTH.

A QUIET heart, submissive, meek,
    Father, do thou bestow,
Which more than granted will not seek
    To have, or give, or know.

Each little hill then holds its gift
    Forth to my joying eyes;
Each mighty mountain will uplift
    My spirit to the skies.

Lo, then the running water sounds
    With gladsome, secret things!
The silent water more abounds,
    And more the hidden springs.

Sweet murmurs then the trees will send
    To hold the birds in song;
The waving grass its tribute lend
    Low music to prolong.

The sun will cast great crowns of light
    On waves that anthems roar;
The dusky billows break at night
    In flashes on the shore.

Yea, every lily's shining cup,
    The hum of hidden bee,
The odours floating mingled up,
    With insect revelry—

All hues, all harmonies divine,
    The holy earth about,
Their souls will send forth into mine,
    My soul to widen out.

And thus the great earth I shall hold,
   A perfect gift of thine;
Richer by these, a thousandfold,
   Than if broad lands were mine.

HYMN FOR A SICK GIRL.

Father, in the dark I lay,
    Thirsting for the light;
Helpless, but for hope alway
    In thy father-might.

Out of darkness came the morn,
    Out of death came life;
I and faith and hope, new-born,
    Out of moaning strife.

So, one morning yet more fair,
    I, alive and brave,
Sudden breathing loftier air,
    Triumph o'er the grave.

HYMN FOR A SICK GIRL.

Though this feeble body lie
    Underneath the ground,
Wide awake, not sleeping, I
    Shall in him be found.

But a morn yet fairer must
    Quell this inner gloom;
Resurrection from the dust
    Of a deeper tomb.

Father, wake thy little child;
    Give me bread and wine,
Till my spirit undefiled
    Rise and live in thine.

A CHRISTMAS CAROL FOR 1862

THE YEAR OF THE TROUBLE IN LANCASHIRE.

The skies are pale, the trees are stiff,
   The earth is dull and old;
The frost is glittering as if
   The very sun were cold.
And hunger fell is joined with frost,
   To make men thin and wan:
Come, babe, from heaven, or we are lost;
   Be born, O child of man.

The children cry, the women shake,
   The strong men stare about;
They sleep when they should be awake,
   They wake ere night is out.

For they have lost their heritage—
  No sweat is on their brow :
Come, babe, and bring them work and wage
  Be born, and save us now.

Across the sea, beyond our sight,
  Roars on the fierce debate ;
The men go down in bloody fight,
  The women weep and hate.
And in the right be which that may,
  Surely the strife is long :
Come, son of man, thy righteous way,
  And right will have no wrong.

Good men speak lies against thine own—
  Tongue quick, and hearing slow ;
They will not let thee walk alone,
  And think to serve thee so :

If they the children's freedom saw
    In thee, the children's king,
They would be still with holy awe,
    Or only speak to sing.

Some neither lie nor starve nor fight,
    Nor yet the poor deny;
But in their hearts all is not right,—
    They often sit and sigh.
We need thee every day and hour,
    In sunshine and in snow:
Child king, we pray with all our power—
    Be born, and save us so.

We are but men and women, Lord;
    Thou art a gracious child;
O fill our hearts, and heap our board,
    Of grace, this winter wild.

And though the trees be sad and bare
 Hunger and hate about,
Come, child, and ill deeds and ill fare
 Will soon be driven out.

A CHRISTMAS CAROL.

Babe Jesus lay in Mary's lap ;
    The sun shone on his hair ;
And this was how she saw, mayhap,
    The crown already there.

For she sang : " Sleep on, my little king;
    Bad Herod dares not come ;
Before thee sleeping, holy thing,
    The wild winds would be dumb.

" I kiss thy hands, I kiss thy feet,
    My child, so long desired ;
Thy hands shall never be soiled, my sweet;
    Thy feet shall never be tired.

"For thou art the king of men, my son;
 Thy crown I see it plain;
And men shall worship thee, every one,
 And cry, Glory! Amen."

Babe Jesus opened his eyes so wide!
 At Mary looked her Lord.
And Mary stinted her song and sighed.
 Babe Jesus said never a word.

THE SLEEPLESS JESUS.

'Tis time to sleep, my little boy;
   Why gaze thy bright eyes so?
At night our children, for new joy,
   Home to thy father go,
But thou are wakeful. Sleep, my child
   The moon and stars are gone;
The wind is up and raving wild;
   But thou art smiling on.

My child, thou hast immortal eyes
   That see by their own light;
They see the children's blood— it lies
   Red-glowing through the night.

Thou hast an ever open ear
  For sob or cry or moan :
Thou seemest not to see or hear,
  Thou only smilest on.

When first thou camest to the earth,
  All sounds of strife were still ;
A silence lay about thy birth,
  And thou didst sleep thy fill.
Thou wakest now—why weep'st thou not ?
  Thy earth is woe-begone ;
Both babes and mothers wail their lot,
  But still thou smilest on.

I read thy face like holy book ;
  No hurt is pictured there ;
Deep in thine eyes I see the look
  Of one who answers prayer.

Beyond pale grief and wild uproars,
    Thou seest God's will well done;
Low prayers, through chambers' closed doors,
    Thou hear'st—and smilest on.

Men say: "I will arise and go."
    God says: "I will go meet."
Thou seest them gather, weeping low,
    About the Father's feet.
And all must, each for others, bear,
    Till all are homeward gone.
Answered, O eyes, ye see all prayer!
    Smile, Son of God, smile on.

THE CHILDREN'S HEAVEN.

The infant lies in blessed ease
    Upon his mother's breast;
No storm, no dark, the baby sees
    Invade his heaven of rest.
He nothing knows of change or death—
    Her face his holy skies;
The air he breathes his mother's breath
    His stars, his mother's eyes.

Yet half the sighs that wander there
    Are born of doubts and fears;
The dew slow falling through that air—
    It is the dew of tears.

And ah! my child, thy heavenly home
    Hath rain as well as dew;
Black clouds fill sometimes all its dome,
    And quench the starry blue.

Her smile would win no smile again,
    If baby saw the things
That ache across his mother's brain,
    The while she sweetly sings.
Thy faith in us is faith in vain—
    We are not what we seem.
O dreary day, O cruel pain,
    That wakes thee from thy dream!

No; pity not his dream so fair,
    Nor fear the waking grief;
Oh, safer he than though we were
    Good as his vague belief!

THE CHILDREN'S HEAVEN.

There is a heaven that heaven above
    Whereon he gazes now;
A truer love than in thy kiss;
    A better friend than thou.

The Father's arms fold like a nest
    His children round about;
His face looks down, a heaven of rest,
    Where comes no dark, no doubt.
Its mists are clouds of stars that move
    In sweet concurrent strife;
Its winds, the goings of his love;
    Its dew, the dew of life.

We for our children seek thy heart,
    For them the Father's eyes:
Lord, when their hopes in us depart,
    Let hopes in thee arise.

When childhood's visions them forsake,
 To women grown and men,
Thou to thy heart their hearts wilt take,
 And bid them dream again.

REJOICE.

"Rejoice," said the Sun; "I will make thee gay
With glory and gladness and holiday;
I am dumb, O man, and I need thy voice."
But man would not rejoice.

"Rejoice in thyself," said he, "O Sun,
For thy daily course is a lordly one;
In thy lofty place, rejoice if thou can·
For me, I am only a man."

"Rejoice," said the Wind; "I am free and strong;
I will wake in thy heart an ancient song;
Hear the roaring woods, my organ noise!"
But man would not rejoice.

"Rejoice, O Wind, in thy strength," said he.
"For thou fulfillest thy destiny;
Shake the forest, the faint flowers fan:
For me, I am only a man."

"Rejoice," said the Night, "with moon and star;
The Sun and the Wind are gone afar;
I am here with rest and dreams of choice."
But man would not rejoice.

For he said—"What is rest to me, I pray,
Whose labour brings no gladsome day?
He only should dream who has hope behind.
Alas for me and my kind!"

Then a voice that came not from moon or star,
From the sun, or the wind roving afar,
Said, "Man, I am with thee— hear my voice."
And man said, "I rejoice."

THE GRACE OF GRACE.

HAD I the grace to win the grace
   Of some old man in lore complete,
My face would worship at his face,
   And I sit lowly at his feet.

Had I the grace to win the grace
   Of childhood, loving shy, apart,
The child should find a nearer place,
   And teach me resting on my heart.

Had I the grace to win the grace
   Of maiden living all above,
My soul would trample down the base,
   That she might have a man to love.

A grace I had no grace to win
   Knocks now at my half-open door:
Ah! Lord of glory, come thou in;—
   Thy grace divine is all, and more!

ANTIPHONY.

Daylight fades away.
  Is the Lord at hand,
In the shadows gray
  Stealing on the land?

  Gently from the east
    Come the shadows gray;
  But our lowly priest
    Nearer is than they.

It is darkness quite.
  Is the Lord at hand,
In the cloak of night
  Stolen upon the land?

But I see no night,
    For my Lord is here;
With him dark is light,
    With him far is near.

List! the cock's awake.
    Is the Lord at hand?
Cometh he to make
    Light in all the land?

Long ago he made
    Morning in my heart;
Long ago he bade
    Shadowy things depart.

Lo, the dawning hill!
    Is the Lord at hand,
Come to scatter ill,
    Ruling in the land?

ANTIPHONY.

He hath scattered ill,
    Ruling in my mind.
Growing to his will.
    Freedom comes, I find.

We will watch all day,
    Lest the Lord should come;
All night waking stay,
    In the darkness dumb.

I will work all day,
    For the Lord hath come;
Down my head will lay,
    All night glad and dumb.

For we know not when
    Christ may be at hand;
But we know that then
    Joy is in the land.

ORGAN SONGS.

    For I know that where
        Christ hath come again,
    Quietness without care
        Dwelleth in his men.

DORCAS.

If I might guess, then guess I would :—
    Amid the gathered folk,
This gentle Dorcas one day stood,
    And heard what Jesus spoke.

She saw the woven seamless coat—
    Half envious for his sake :
" Oh, happy hands," she said, " that wrought
    That honoured thing to make ! "

Her eyes with longing tears grow dim
    She never can come nigh
To work one service poor for him
    For whom she glad would die !

But hark! he speaks a mighty word:
  She hearkens now indeed!
" When did we see thee naked, Lord,
  And clothed thee in thy need?

" The King shall answer, Inasmuch
  As to my brothers ye
Did it—even to the least of such—
  Ye did it unto me."

Home, home she went, and plied the loom
  And Jesus' poor arrayed.
She died—they wept about the room,
  And showed the coats she made.

MARRIAGE SONG.

"They have no more wine," she said.
But they had enough of bread;
And the vessels by the door
Held for thirst a plenteous store:
Yes, *enough;* but Love divine
Turned the water into wine.

When should wine not water flow,
But when home two glad hearts go,
And in sacred bondage bound,
Soul in soul hath freedom found?

Meetly then, a holy sign,
Turns the water into wine.

Good is all the feasting then :
Good the merry words of men ;
Good the laughter and the smiles ;
Good the wine that grief beguiles ;—
Crowning good, the Word divine
Turning water into wine.

Friends, the Master with you dwell :
Daily work this miracle ;
When fair things too common grow
Wake again the heavenly show :
Ever at your table dine,
Turning water into wine.

So at last you shall descry
All the patterns of the sky :

Earth a heaven of short abode ;
Houses temples unto God ;
Waterpots, to vision fine,
Brimming full of heavenly wine.

BLIND BARTIMEUS.

As Jesus went into Jericho town,
'Twas darkness all, from toe to crown,
    About blind Bartimeus.
He said, "When eyes are so very dim,
They are no use for seeing him;
    No matter—he can see us.

"Cry out, cry out, blind brother—cry;
    Let not salvation dear go by.—
        Have mercy, Son of David."
Though they were blind, they both could hear—
They heard, and cried, and he drew near;
    And so the blind were saved.

BLIND BARTIMEUS.

O Jesus Christ, I am very blind;
Nothing comes through into my mind;
   'Tis well I am not dumb:
Although I see thee not, nor hear,
I cry because thou may'st be near:
   O son of Mary, come.

I hear it through the all things blind:
Is it thy voice, so gentle and kind—
   " Poor eyes, no more be dim "?
A hand is laid upon mine eyes;
I hear, and hearken, see, and rise—
   'Tis He: I follow him.

COME UNTO ME.

Come unto me, the Master says,
   But how? I am not good;
No thankful song my heart will raise,
   Nor even wish it could.

I am not sorry for the past,
   Nor able not to sin;
The weary strife would ever last
   If once I should begin.

Hast thou no burden then to bear?
   No action to repent?
Is all around so very fair?
   Is thy heart quite content?

COME UNTO ME.

Hast thou no sickness in thy soul?
    No labour to endure?
Then go in peace, for thou art whole:
    Thou needest not his cure.

Ah! mock me not. Sometimes I sigh;
    I have a nameless grief,
A faint sad pain—but such that I
    Can look for no relief.

Come, come to him who made thy heart;
    Come weary and oppressed;
To come to Jesus is thy part,
    His part to give thee rest.

New grief, new hope he will bestow
    Thy grief and pain to quell;
Into thy heart himself will go,
    And that will make thee well.

MORNING HYMN.

O Lord of life, thy quickening voice
   Awakes my morning song;
In gladsome words I would rejoice
   That I to thee belong.

I see thy light, I feel thy wind;
   Earth is thy uttered word;
Whatever wakes my heart and mind,
   Thy presence is, my Lord.

The living soul which I call me
   Doth love, and long to know;
It is a thought of living thee,
   Nor forth of thee can go.

Therefore I choose my highest part,
    And turn my face to thee ;
Therefore I stir my inmost heart
    To worship fervently.

Lord, let me live and act this day,
    Still rising from the dead ;
Lord, make my spirit good and gay—
    Give me my daily bread.

Within my heart, speak, Lord, speak on,
    My heart alive to keep,
Till the night comes, and, labour done,
    In thee I fall asleep.

NOONTIDE.

I LOVE thy skies, thy sunny mists,
    Thy fields, thy mountains hoar,
Thy wind that bloweth where it lists—
    Thy will, I love it more.

I love thy hidden truth to seek
    All round, in sea, on shore;
The arts whereby like gods we speak—
    Thy will to me is more.

I love thy men and women, Lord,
    The children round thy door,
Calm thoughts that inward strength afford—
    Thy will, O Lord, is more.

But when thy will my life shall hold
    Thine to the very core,
The world, which that same will did mould,
    I shall love ten times more.

EVENING HYMN.

O God, whose daylight leadeth down
   Into the sunless way,
Who with restoring sleep dost crown
   The labour of the day!

What I have done, Lord, make it clean
   With thy forgiveness dear;
That so to-day what might have been,
   To-morrow may appear.

And when my thought is all astray,
   Yet think thou on in me;
That with the new-born innocent day
   My soul rise fresh and free.

Nor let me wander all in vain
   Through dreams that mock and flee;
But even in visions of the brain,
   Go wandering towards thee.

THE HOLY MIDNIGHT.

Ah, holy midnight of the soul,
   When stars alone are high;
When winds are resting at their goal,
   And sea-waves only sigh!

Ambition faints from out the will;
   Asleep sad longing lies;
All hope of good, all fear of ill,
   All need of action dies;

Because God is; and claims the life
   He kindled in thy brain;
And thou in him, rapt far from strife,
   Diest and liv'st again.

END OF VOL. II.

www.ingramcontent.com/pod-product-compliance
Lightning Source LLC
Chambersburg PA
CBHW032047230426
43672CB00009B/1507